INSIGHTS ON
IMPLEMENTATION

TPM

COLLECTED PRACTICES & CASES

PRODUCTIVITY PRESS

New York, New York

Most Productivity Press books are available at quantity discounts when purchased in bulk. For more information contact our Customer Service Department (888-319-5852). Address all other inquiries to:

Productivity Press
444 Park Avenue South, 7th Floor
New York, NY 10016
United States of America
Telephone: 212-686-5900
Fax: 212-686-5411
E-mail: info@productivitypress.com

Material originally appeared in the *Lean Manufacturing Advisor*, 1999-2005.

Library of Congress Cataloging-in-Publication Date

08 07 06 05 9 8 7 6 5 4 3 2 1

Contents

Introduction

Equipment downtime can bring a lean manufacturing operation to a complete standstill. In a pull system with continuous flow, the failure of equipment at one step of a process halts all the steps before it. An operator can only pull work from a preceding step when he is able to perform that work.

That is why total productive maintenance (TPM) is such a fundamental part of becoming lean. Strategies aimed at eliminating downtime are essential in any operation where the processes require the use of equipment.

As with all aspects of lean, implementing TPM is not easy. Learning how different companies have approached this challenge can provide insights useful in developing your own strategies.

The chapters in this book were originally published as articles in *Lean Manufacturing Advisor,* a newsletter that each month chronicles how companies are implementing lean production. The case studies and expert advice you will find here can serve as a source of information, knowledge and inspiration as you move forward on your own TPM journey.

This book is divided into three sections. The first part describes several strategies not only in regard to the general implementation

---

[1] For more information regarding the articles in this book, including the original dates of publication, please refer to the citations section.

of TPM but also for measuring the success and effectiveness of your TPM efforts.

In the second section, the focus is on the management and cultural challenges that confront any business embracing TPM. These chapters provide examples of ways to train people in TPM, overcome initial failures and put in place policies and procedures that will help sustain your implementation well into the future.

Overall equipment effectiveness (OEE), a key metric for any equipment-based process, is the topic of the final section of this book. Practical issues and strategic application of OEE are covered in these chapters.

The real-world experiences you will encounter in these pages can serve as a practical companion to other books that cover the precise methodologies of implementing TPM. They may also inspire you and perhaps make your lean journey a little smoother.

Ralph Bernstein
Editor
Lean Manufacturing Advisor

Part I

Strategies for TPM

OVERVIEW

TPM efforts should not be conducted at random. As with other lean practices, they should be based on clear strategy and measured with clear metrics that are easy to implement and understand. The chapters in this section describe approaches that can be taken to provide a TPM initiative with the proper direction.

IMC Chemicals set the unusual goal of cost-cutting for its TPM program, rather than increasing uptime, with the primary focus on TPM rather than lean overall. What the company did, and how its results were different from expectations, is described in Chapter 1.

Ogihara America recognized the importance of having comprehensive data, clear goals and an organizational structure to support TPM activities. Chapter 2 relates how its strategy achieved both benefits and recognition.

The bottom line matters for all businesses. The approach of National Semiconductor is to measure TPM success not just in terms of uptime, but also in money saved by reducing losses. Learn how they did it in Chapter 3.

Kaiser Aluminum is also interested in money. Their strategy, explained in Chapter 4, is to calculate the return on investment from TPM activities, taking into account the many different ways in which TPM can reduce costs.

The concept of reliability centered maintenance (RCM) is presented in Chapter 5. RCM is used by Whirlpool to complement its TPM efforts by identifying the best opportunities for improvement. That is achieved by applying specific criteria to determine those opportunities.

Chapter 6 deals with what might seem to be a contradiction in terms: maintenance of maintenance-free parts. But Agilent

Technologies recognized that even so-called maintenance-free parts require maintenance of the environment in which they are located.

And Chapter 7 explains how the autonomous maintenance aspects of TPM, as well as 5S, can be applied in an unlikely environment — by a municipal parks department.

1

TPM Takes Center Stage
At California Chemical Plant

September, 2002

Total productive maintenance (TPM) is usually one part of a broader lean initiative, and its goal is usually to improve equipment uptime and reliability.

At the IMC Chemicals site in the Searles Valley of California, the usual practices are turned upside down. The TPM effort there — named Basic Equipment Care (BEC) — is not only the cornerstone of a lean transformation but an umbrella concept covering all other lean initiatives. And ironically, the program got started not to improve reliability, but to save money.

Money has been saved in the four years since the effort began. But perhaps more importantly, downtime has decreased (along with overtime), maintenance costs have gone down, and IMC has transitioned to an entirely different way of operating. Maintenance crews spend more time on preventive measures as opposed to emergencies, employees are now enthusiastic members of teams, and previously isolated departments are learning to work together. In addition, the facility is shipping more product than before.

"The cost-cutting started to happen, but the other results that we got are probably the ones we really enjoy more than the cost-cutting," says Pam Allen, maintenance process development engineer for IMC. "People are allowed to go out and work on things that are really important to them."

"They have got to a point in their journey that not many people ever get to," observes Ellis New, a Productivity, Inc., consultant who has worked with IMC. "They've just continued to raise the bar themselves. They've gone further in the journey than a lot of people do. I marvel at what they've done."

Equipment Is Critical

IMC Chemicals is headquartered in Overland Park, Kan., and has operations in California, Colorado and Italy. The company mines and processes chemicals that include borax, boric acid, soda ash, sodium bicarbonate, sodium sulfate and specialty borates.

The California location is in the middle of nowhere. Five facilities sit in the Searles Valley in lower California on the high-desert remains of an ancient lake — a site rich in the chemicals the company seeks. The buildings have their own power plant. The closest services are a two-hour drive away.

Material is mined and combined with liquid to form a slurry. (It is one of the few warm-solution mining operations in the world.) The liquid is pumped into the different buildings and processed into finished, dry chemicals.

It's an equipment-intensive business, and the equipment is from 25 to 100 years old, says Allen, adding, "There are massive amounts of deterioration that we deal with here. Our maintenance department was overwhelmed. They were having a tendency to spend all their time on emergencies and major crises, and didn't have much time allocated to spend on minor stuff."

New diplomatically describes IMC in 1998 as "a target-rich environment. There was no bad place to start because there was so much opportunity for improvement. Their people are wonderful folks, but they had worked and survived in those conditions for a long time."

Before (top) and after pictures show how the condition of pumps at IMC Chemicals in California has improved under the company's Basic Equipment Care program.

In 1998, "we had been instructed from our corporate folks to come up with some way to reduce our maintenance costs," Allen explains. After some initial work with a first consultant whose suggestions "didn't fit the nature of our plant very well," executives attended a Productivity workshop on autonomous maintenance.

IMC then moved to have several of its people trained as trainers. "We have now certified a total of five people," notes New. "They have taken our material and made it their material. Their process is really a benchmark."

A Better Environment

Allen notes a broad range of improvements that have resulted from the BEC program, including solving problems of spillage and leakage, as well as making equipment easier to operate.

For example, "over the years, our culture allowed spillage to happen. We just tolerated and accepted fairly significant amounts of spillage." This occurred, she notes, because the products are non-toxic and because "we are a process plant. If one piece of equipment goes down, the whole plant goes down. One minor spill really doesn't cost nearly as much as if you took a piece of equipment down and fixed it."

However, with BEC, "our teams have been incredibly creative. They figured out how to get in there and fix these spillage issues without impacting production."

In one case, a team tackled the problem of spillage on railroad tracks. (Tracks run throughout the site, then connect with a main line.) "The team actually figured out how to make a new bucket device to go on a loader so they could run the loader down the track and clean product off the track," Allen explains. The new device, developed for one part of the facility, was then also used for other areas.

Instituting regular equipment checks and audits uncovered some scary problems. In the on-site power generator, "a lot of the plant is run by remote. When they looked at the interlocks, they found that one of the safety overrides had not been installed, and nobody knew that. If we had a plant upset, the scrubber unit would not have kicked on the sprays to protect it, and it would have melted down," she states, adding that such a disaster might have caused $100,000 in damage.

Another team reviewed the operations of a set of three pumps. "Two of the three had certain efficiencies," Allen says. "The third was dramatically lower. We would never have found it if we hadn't gone through and done a basic audit process. That's helped the whole efficiency of the plant. It's one of those hidden defects. The pump was running, but we didn't know the efficiency level was so low."

Total Involvement

Throughout the program, IMC has been striving to avoid moves that might upset employees. For example, the phrase "autonomous maintenance" was abandoned in favor of Basic Equipment Care because "the word autonomous terrified everybody," Allen declares.

For similar reasons, she notes, while other lean tools such as visual controls and 5S have been implemented at IMC, "they have all been brought under the BEC umbrella. When we look like we are doing a program-of-the-month thing, people get very upset about it." The additional lean tools, she suggests, might be referred to as "advanced BEC."

Allen advises others who might pursue a TPM program to "make sure that you involve your entire plant. It's not just a manage-ment process. It's not just an employee process. Everyone has to participate."

She also suggests that "it will work a whole lot better if you build teams as you implement this process." And she stresses that "your leadership folks need to understand that the command-and-con-trol things don't work very well. You really have to take on more of a coaching and mentoring role."

New praises Allen and her colleagues for "not being willing to take no for an answer. They faced obstacles up front that would have made anybody say 'I give up.'"

While any TPM program should be ongoing, "you need to go back and reflect on what you've done," Allen notes. "The teams have a tendency to get a project done and go forward. They can get so bogged down with issues they have currently, they forget how much they've actually accomplished. They can get kind of depressed."

And she offers one final piece of advice: "Make sure you get 'before' pictures. You cannot understand the value of a 'before' picture until about a year later."

TAKEAWAYS

- TPM can be the centerpiece of a lean initiative, not just a small part.
- Implementing TPM may reveal long-standing problems and poor practices.
- Choosing the right name for the initiative can be important.

2

Data Drives
Maintenance Effort

April, 2004

The key to a successful total productive maintenance program is not the actual maintenance activities. Sustaining an effective program depends on everything that supports those activities: collection of accurate data, scorecards that show the significance of the data, clearly defined responsibilities for everyone involved, and procedures that provide for ongoing support of TPM efforts.

That philosophy lies behind the approach at Japanese-owned Ogihara America Corporation, a supplier of automotive body parts with plants in Howell, Mich. and Birmingham, Ala. It's a philosophy that, in six years, has taken a company with no TPM program to become one whose program has not only raised machine efficiency and increased capacity, but has also won recognition.

For example, in 2001, the Howell plant was one of a number of companies awarded a TPM excellence award by JIPM, the Japan Institute of Plant Maintenance, a consortium of companies backed by the Japanese government and dedicated to promoting Japanese economic growth by spreading the gospel of TPM. The Birmingham plant won a similar award in 2003.

Structure, Definitions and Data

Ogihara launched its TPM effort in 1998 to cope with success. At that time, its plants were operating at full capacity — 24/7 — and

9

TPM was seen as a way to boost capacity by reducing equipment downtime.

Working with JIPM consultants, the company initially developed a "road map" for TPM, laying out how to integrate TPM efforts into Ogihara's operating system, according to Tony Dunker, TPM coordinator at the Howell plant, which employs close to 600 people.

Since then, the company has developed a clear structure for addressing TPM. There are dedicated positions — at Howell, for example, these include Dunker, autonomous maintenance coordinator Brian Kaitner, and others — as well as clearly defined TPM responsibilities for such positions as facilitator, team leader, and others (see sidebar next page).

In a parallel move, Ogihara has created what it calls a set of cascading goals and objectives. These range from annual objectives and quarterly reviews at the level of the president and operating committee, down through manufacturing objectives for the directors and executive managers, departmental objectives and cost center objectives.

Meetings are also a part of the process. There are regularly scheduled weekly meetings to address problem areas, plus monthly reviews to follow up on progress and to understand the condition of each area. And of course, actual maintenance activities are scheduled at regular times.

No less important is the handling of TPM-related data, something that evolved over time. Ogihara collects and stores company data with business software from QAD, and "we weren't really utilizing that data the way we should," Dunker notes. "We couldn't tell you half the things we could tell you now, as far as machine efficiency, downtime, maintenance requirements."

With the launch of a TPM philosophy, he adds, "we started out taking a look at where our major failures were, and what types of failures. We would do a five-why analysis." At the same time, employees were being trained to figure out how to solve TPM problems.

Who Is Responsible for What

Ogihara's TPM program defines employee responsibilities at four levels: executive manager, manager, facilitator and team leader.

For all levels except facilitator, the position's primary job function is defined, as well as the principle duties and responsibilities. Because of the unique nature of the facilitator position, the job is defined in terms of "basic functions." In addition, expectations are clearly stated for the facilitator and team leader.

For example, the executive manager's functions include developing and administering procedures and policies, directing manufacturing, supporting development of cost objectives and supporting development of all associates. The principal duties and responsibilities cover related items, such as managing operating costs and overseeing the budget process.

The manager administers the policies and procedures, as well as also being involved in directing manufacturing and supporting development efforts. Duties and responsibilities are also similar to those of the executive manager.

The facilitator's functions, which are focused on human resource management, include development of teams, planning and executing daily activities, managing manpower, equipment and materials efficiently, maintaining/improving safety and housekeeping, as well as functions related to customer service, ISO/QS processes and product launches.

The team leader assigns and directs associates, verifies material usage, downtime, and product quality, etc.

Both facilitators and team leaders are expected to drive action, activity and accountability in their respective areas, as well as drive continuous improvement efforts. Detailed lists of other expectations are also delineated.

To bring it all together, the company created a series of scorecards, with different cards for different levels. There is an overall company scorecard (a portion of which is shown on the next page), department scorecards and line scorecards. Each card clearly states the metrics being used, along with the areas that must be improved in order to support company goals.

QOS Objective Performance Scorecard
OAC Manufacturing Operations Objectives - Howell — Person Reporting: Ray Ziegler

	Objective	Benchmark	Target	Apr	May	Jun	Jul	Aug	Sept	Oct	Nov	Dec	Jan	Feb	March	Annual
Safety	**Manufacturing Overall**															
	# of Incidents		Target	0	0	0	0	0	0	0	0	0	0	0	0	
			Actual	8	8	7	3	2	2	6	4	4	4	6	0	
	Lost time		Target	0	0	0	0	0	0	0	0	0	0	0	0	
			Actual	24	4	180	4	0	0	61	0	0	58	41	0	
	Restricted time		Target	0	0	0	0	0	0	0	0	0	0	0	0	
			Actual	3	64	77	4	65	5	63	22	17	110	56	0	
Quality	**Customer Concerns Quality**															
	Wixom PPM		Target	500	500	500	500	500	500	500	500	500	500	500	500	
			Actual	510	333	218	686	875	639	0	18	42	0	0		
	Chrysler PPM		Target	50	50	50	50	50	50	50	50	50	50	50	50	
			Actual	0	8	0	0	0	29	25	0	0	0	0	4	
	Other PPM		Target	50	50	50	50	50	50	50	50	50	50	50	50	
			Actual	21	18	18	18	18	18	18	18	18	18	18	18	
	Number of Customer Concerns		Target	18	18	18	18	18	18	18	18	18	18	18		
			Actual	11	11	8	5	18	2	4	8	8	13	13		
	Internal Quality															
	Dimensional CP % of Pts >1.33		Target	85.0%	85.0%	85.0%	85.0%	85.0%	85.0%	85.0%	85%	85%	85%	85%	85%	
			Actual	59.0%	58.0%	64.0%	51.0%	69%	61.0%	63.0%	69%	72%	73%	72%	72%	
	Dimensional CPK % of pts >1.00		Target	60.0%	60.0%	60.0%	60.0%	60.0%	60.0%	60.0%	60%	60%	60%	60%	60%	
			Actual	58.0%	26.0%	33.0%	38.0%	35.0%	34.0%	35.0%	40%	42%	42%	45%	44%	
	Weld Capability		Target	98.0%	98.0%	98.0%	98.0%	98.0%	98.0%	98.0%	98%	98%	98%	98%	98%	
			Actual	99.9%	99.9%	99.9%	99.9%	99.9%	99.9%	99.4%	99.0%	99.98%	99.99%	99.99%	99.99%	
	Quality Percentage		Target	95%	95.0%	95%	95%	95%	95%	95%	95%	95%	95%	95%	95%	
			Actual	98.0%	97.0%	98%	98%	97%	98.0%	98.0%	98.0%	98.3%	98.0%	95.8%		
Cost	**Budget**															
	Manufacturing Area		Target	89%	83%	86%	107%	86.76%	90	86	90	98	90	89		
			Actual	92%	92%	90%	117%	124.47%	106.5	97.0	98%	102%	102%	92%		
	Cost of Sales Percentage		Target	1%	1%	1%	1%	1%	1%	1%	1%	1%	1%	1%	1%	
			Actual													
	Scrap % (% of sales)		Target	1%	1%	1%	1%	2%	2%	2%	2%	2%	2%	2%	1%	
			Actual													
	Scrap % (Production)		Target	1%	1%	1%	1%	1%	1%	1%	1%	1%	1%	1%	1%	
			Actual	0.76%	0.82%	0.54%	0.49%	0.48%	1.17%	5.10%	0.87%	0.70%	0.81%	1.54%		
	Press															
	1500 Ton SPM	11.22	Target	12.70	12.78	12.87	12.95	13.04	13.12	13.21	13.28	13.37	13.45	13.54	13.60	
			Actual	10.28	9.75	8.81	9.77	9.86	11.64	10.82	7.64	7.38	10.92	11.93	12.13	
	2700 Ton SPM	7.06	Target	7.73	7.80	7.87	7.94	8.01	8.08	8.15	8.22	8.30	8.66	9.03	9.40	
			Actual	6.46	6.80	7.42	7.00	7.46	6.67	6.39	5.25	6.29	5.50	9.03	8.39	
	A-Line SPM	3.73	Target	4.91	4.95	5.00	5.04	5.08	5.13	5.17	5.25	5.26	5.31	5.36	5.40	
			Actual	4.39	4.85	5.11	4.76	4.91	4.15	3.78	3.63	4.69	4.38	4.14	4.23	
	B-Line SPM	3.73	Target	3.34	3.40	3.46	3.52	3.58	3.64	3.70	3.76	3.82	3.88	3.94	4.00	

(Row labels at far left, reading bottom to top: Safety, Quality, Cost, Manufacturing Overall)

Different colors are used to highlight different scores, red being used for those most in need of improvement. "Any area that has more than two months in red, not meeting its target, the manager will get involved," explains Dunker. "Any area that has three months in red, the (supervisor) next level up will get involved. By doing that, the folks have the support they need. By getting the folks at the higher levels involved, we're holding them accountable for their areas."

It took some time to get to this point, Dunker recalls: "Each year we're able to identify areas as far as data collection and accuracy of the data. Once we got into the data, accuracy became a question. After we started digging into it, we found out a lot of things that were just kind of out in space — nobody was really taking responsibility for them. Specifically, downtime reasons, scrap reasons. Nobody was addressing that because it never had a home. Now we make sure we have all the scrap codes, all the downtime codes. All the areas are covered by someone having ownership or responsibility for every bit of data."

He adds that the approach at Ogihara was inspired partly by a visit he and others made to a Harley-Davidson plant. "I was very impressed that people at the shop floor level knew what it cost to paint a motorcycle frame," he recalls.

The years of effort have produced results. For example, "we've raised machine efficiency in the assembly department about 20 percent. We're pushing 95 to 98 percent," Dunker boasts.

He concludes, "I think the big thing is, we've gotten information out to the associate level as to what the things are that they can do and work on. We're giving them knowledge and documents that are easy for them to use."

TAKEAWAYS

- A successful TPM effort requires ongoing data collection and analysis.
- Job responsibilities must be clearly defined for all involved in TPM.
- Metrics must be appropriate, with clear trigger points for action.

3

TPM Theme:
Show Me the Money

March, 2003

Les Gardner follows the money.

As TPM manager for the National Semiconductor plant in South Portland, Maine, Gardner helps determine where plant employees will focus their efforts to improve operations and reduce losses.

Total productive maintenance programs typically revolve around the metric of overall equipment effectiveness (OEE), which is derived from a formula involving availability, standard run rate and first-pass quality.

But at the National Semiconductor Maine plant — where TPM is an umbrella management system for continuous improvement — executives calculate the dollar impact of every loss they identify. That calculation is used to prioritize improvement efforts.

Determining the dollar impact is important for two reasons, Gardner maintains. First, the importance of a loss may vary with business conditions. Cost reduction may be a major focus during slow times, for example, while yield or productivity loss may be more important during boom times.

Second, some losses are hard to identify. Situations where significant scrap is generated or where someone gets hurt are "the big hitters, the most visible and perhaps the easiest to justify devoting resources to," Gardner says.

But "there are a lot of other losses out there," and "if you don't have a structured approach (to identifying losses), you leave a lot of money on the table." Gardner described the TPM program during Productivity's 7th Annual Lean Management & TPM Conference.

The National Semiconductor program has been expanding and evolving since its launch in Maine in 1998. It has produced benefits in a range of areas, Gardner says, from equipment restoration to equipment failures to office information systems and even to new product introductions. And the process being followed, he maintains, can be adapted and used by virtually any company (see sidebar below).

How to Make it Work

To apply the National Semiconductor approach to your company, TPM Manager Les Gardner suggests the following:

1. Translate the 16 major losses into the language of your industry and factory.
2. Develop a macro site loss report and reporting frequency.
3. Assign loss categories to the owners of each TPM program element or pillar.
4. Develop metrics for each loss.
5. Quantify and dollarize the losses.
6. Prioritize opportunities based on dollar impact and state of the business.
7. Launch improvement teams to drive losses to zero.
8. Recognize success.

The first point, translating the losses, involves defining what a loss is and offering examples. In translating losses for the semiconductor industry, Gardner notes that National Semiconductor defines a failure loss as "time lost when equipment fails," with examples including robot failure, a broken drive belt or a chiller leak.

A category of cutting blade loss is defined as "time lost in shutdown to change consumables, start up and stabilize process." Examples are polishing pads and conditioning wheels.

Pillars of Support

The Maine plant, which employs 570 people, is only a small part of National Semiconductor. However, its progress in improving operations parallels the company's overall results. For the quarter ending Nov. 24, 2002, National Semiconductor reported a net profit of $6.2 million on revenues of $422.3 million. That compares with a loss of $46.6 million on revenues of $366.4 million a year earlier.

The foundation of the Maine TPM program consists of eight pillar steering groups (PSGs). Each of these is responsible for one of nine pillars of TPM at the Maine plant:

- Environmental, Health and Safety
- Autonomous Maintenance
- Planned Maintenance
- Focused Improvement
- Education and Training
- Initial Phase Management
- Business Support
- Quality Maintenance, and Leadership Development

Each PSG is led by a senior staff member and is responsible for understanding and reducing losses within its area. This includes measuring and reporting them once a month, and launching and monitoring the work of improvement teams. Major losses are identified twice a year using a matrix of 16 major losses (see diagram, page 18). (The number may be flexible; Gardner spoke at the conference of 16 losses, but his matrix listed 18.)

All losses are ultimately converted into dollars, but that calculation is based on other metrics, including numbers of injuries, wafers scrapped, interruptions, etc. And in fact, Gardner says, managers at the Maine plant do measure OEE on individual machines.

How the conversion is calculated depends on the loss. Scrap is fairly straightforward. The cost of injuries might be calculated

Site Priorities		Loss #	Major Loss Types	PR Pillar	Top Two Opportunities	Loss Metric (Last 6 Periods)	Total $(K) Loss (Last 6 Periods)
1. Safety	EHS	1	Worker Injuries	EHS	Lost Time Hours	# hr	$
					Restricted Duty Hours	# hr	$
2. Quality	Quality	2	Quality Incidents	QM	Process	# Wafers	$
					Process	# Wafers	
		3	Design Related Yield — Design for Manufactuability	QM	Product	$	$
					Product	$	
		4	New Process/Equipment Introduction	IPM	Material	#	$
					Product	#	$
					Schedule Push Out	$	
2. Quality Yields	Yield (cum/cum)	5	Human Related (Fab Yield)	E&T	ET Related Scrap	$	$
					MT Related Scrap	$	
		6	Tool Failure (Fab Yield)	PM	Defect Area	# Wafers	$
					Defect Area	# Wafers	
		7	Ys (Die Yield)	FI	Defect Area	% Die	$
					Defect Area	% Die	
		8	Yd (Die Yield)	FI	Defect Area	% Die	$
		9	ET/Sort Survival	FI	Defect Type	# Wafers	$
		10	Facilities (All Interuptions)	EHS	Facility/IS Interuption	# Interuption	$
					Energy	# MBTU	$
	Spending Losses	11	Cost/Layer Spending	BS	Fixed: Service Contracts	$/Layer	$
					Fixed: Depreciation/Taxes	$/Layer	$
					Variable: $/L	ayer	
					Variable	$/Layer	
		12	Productivity	AM	Direct Labor	# hr	$
				PM	SNE Productivity	# hr	$
				BS	Exempt	%	$
3. Activity Cost	Capacity & Cycle Time for Top 5 Constraints: Tool A, Tool B, Tool C, Tool D, Tool E	13	Equipment Failure, Consumables, Planned Shutdown Beyond Entitlement (availability)	PM	Process	%	$
		14	Minor Stoppages/Idling (Efficiency)	PM	Process	%	$
					Process	%	$
		15	Speed (UPH)	FI	Process	# UPH	$
					Process	# UPH	$
		16	Rework (%)	FI	Process	%	$
					Process	%	$
	Skills Loss	17	Retention	E&T	Attrition	# Employees	$
					Attrition	# Employees	$
		18	Skills	E&T	MT gap to 100% Productive	$	$
					ET gap to 100% Productive	$	$
					SNE Emergency Support	$	

Total Loss:

*Updated at Mid Year

National Semiconductor uses a major loss matrix, shown here, to identify, assess, and prioritize areas for improvement.

18

with overtime and medical expenses. A staffing shortage, or a situation where some workers do not have all required skills, involves different calculations (see sidebar below).

The overall goal is simple: zero losses, meaning zero breakdowns, zero scrap, and zero injuries. Setting perfection as a goal, Gardner says, "keeps you thinking out of the box."

Eliminating Scrap

In an example presented at the conference, Gardner said that scrap caused by human error was identified as a major loss. Two pillar steering groups — education and training, and manufacturing and engineering — worked together to reduce this loss.

A first step was to update procedures for dealing with problems, known as OCAPs — Out of Control Action Plans. Process variation root causes were also eliminated, which reduced the number of OCAPs and their complexity.

Manufacturing technicians were barred from running tools in manual mode, and the discipline of using automated OCAPs was reinforced.

How to Calculate a Skills Loss

When a manufacturing process at National Semiconductor requires 60 manufacturing technicians, and only 50 are available, that's a gap of 10. Assume the average worker costs $20 per hour (wages and benefits) and works a 40-hour week, or a cost of $800 per week. Multiply that by 4 to get the cost per month, then by 10 for the total worker shortage. The result is that the shortage of 10 workers costs the company $32,000 per month.

Now assume further that the 50 workers who are present are only at a 70 percent skill level, meaning a skills gap of 30 percent. Take the $800 cost per worker per week, multiply it by 4 to get the cost per month. Take 30 percent of that figure and multiply it by 50 workers. The result is a skills loss of $48,000 per month.

Therefore, when you add the two figures together, the total cost of the skills and staffing shortage is $80,000 per month.

A new training program was developed with improved specifications and other materials. Computer-based training was utilized, and technicians were certified after completing training.

The improvements were implemented in January of 2002. Since then, there have been no incidents of employee-related scrap.

In a report at the conference, Gardner wrote that "in making these improvements, an underlying theme of TPM is realized. The process was stabilized and improved to the point of being more predictable. At this new level of performance, personnel are freed from hectic, non-value-added tasks...

"The whole activity of reducing scrap losses heightened the awareness of all involved. This created a concerted team effort to eliminate the losses... Now, no one wants to be the one to spoil the zero manufacturing technician scrap record."

Talking the Talk

Gardner stresses that "an aggressive cost-reduction goal is necessary to focus the organization on purposefully attacking losses. Loss reduction is a continuous focus rather than an informal, as-needed process."

However, he also boasts that significant progress has been made at the Maine plant, where employees now see a problem and say "we'll TPM that."

"That's when you know it's really working," he says. "It becomes part of your vocabulary."

TAKEAWAYS

- Calculating the dollar impact of every equipment-related loss can help prioritize improvement efforts.
- Different measures and calculations may be needed for calculating the impact of different types of losses.
- Losses may be categorized as either quality yield issues or activity costs.

4

You Can Measure the ROI Produced by TPM Efforts

July, 2000

Total productive maintenance (TPM) is not just a way of improving machine reliability. It's an investment in your company that produces significant benefits — which can and should be measured.

That's the philosophy of David Frye, TPM director for Kaiser Aluminum, who contends that understanding those benefits can help convince executives and operators of the value of TPM. He argues that TPM can be looked at like any other corporate investment with a measurable return on that investment.

At the same time, Frye — who came to Kaiser recently from Kodak — notes that not all benefits of TPM can be predicted. To some extent, he says, managers will have to have faith that the benefits will appear. However, they will appear within a very short time, he says.

"The original consulting spend/benefit curve is that you're going to invest money, and in a year to 18 months, you'll see a return," Frye states. "In this economy, nobody's going to invest money and wait 18 months. If you don't get a return in 6 months, you're doing it wrong. If you're not at a breakeven point in a month, you've probably selected the wrong piece of equipment, or you've gone about it wrong."

A Range of Benefits

The actual investment in getting TPM started, Frye contends, is relatively small. "It shouldn't cost you a whole lot," he says. "If you're spending a lot, you're doing it wrong."

He describes the costs as typically including:

- $6,000 to $15,000 for consulting services.

- An increase of up to 10 percent in maintenance materials during the first 6 months.

- Two to five shifts of production time during the initial implementation period, as well as weekly maintenance time. Frye cautions, "Never try to do the whole plant at once." Targeting one piece of equipment at a time is preferable.

- Training for all personnel.

The success of TPM is typically measured in terms of improved machine performance — increased uptime, fewer breakdowns, longer-lasting parts, all of which lead to increased production.

However, during his experience at Kodak, where TPM was initiated in mid-2000, Frye said a number of additional benefits, some unintended, were also produced:

For example, **unit manufacturing** cost dropped significantly within a year as a result of TPM.

Maintenance overtime initially spikes upward, then drops significantly as TPM becomes standard operating procedure. "If you're implementing at the right rate, the spike will be pretty short-lived," says Frye. At Kodak, overtime had been running at a rate of 15 to 20 percent, but TPM enabled the company to bring it down to around 10 percent.

Similarly, **maintenance costs,** which had been running close to or slightly above budgeted amounts, dropped to below the budget allocation.

Meanwhile, **employee absenteeism** fell from rates of between 2.5 to 3 percent down to below 2 percent 2 years later.

Also, **maintenance customer satisfaction** jumped significantly. The operators on the shop floor are considered the customers of maintenance. Their satisfaction was measured at Kodak through a survey consisting of three questions: Was maintenance proactive, with maintenance personnel coming around without being called? Do they fix equipment properly and explain what they did? Do they check back with you in some period of time to make sure the equipment is running to your satisfaction? "Before we started TPM, the scores were pretty horrible," Frye admits.

Maintenance stores inventory, meaning spare parts for equipment, also declined. "Depending on the complexity of your operation, you could have well over a million dollars worth of spare parts," Frye warns. "If equipment is properly maintained, you don't need that many spare parts."

Mean Time to Restore (MTTR), meaning the average amount of time it takes to get a machine back in production after a breakdown, is another measure of TPM effectiveness because shortening MTTR increases production time. "You can measure reliability basically two ways," Frye explains. "If the goal is production time, you can improve that by shortening the amount of time a machine is down. If you were averaging 10 minutes and now you are averaging 5 minutes, for example. The other way is to improve the mean time between failures. If it was once an hour and you improve to once every 2 hours, that goes back into production."

Effective TPM also can reduce the need for maintenance personnel, who Frye says are often hard to find because manufacturing industries face a shortage of good maintenance people.

Faith in the Unexpected

Frye also makes the point that virtually every TPM effort will produce unexpected benefits. At one Kodak facility, for example,

TPM was used to address leaks in systems that supplied compressed air. By solving the problem, use of compressed air dropped by more than 30 percent — along with the cost of that air.

Another unexpected benefit was that, following implementation of TPM, the numbers of past due orders and backorders dropped dramatically. "Did we set out with TPM to reduce backorders? No," Frye says.

At Kaiser, TPM efforts targeting a sawing machine reduced from three to one the number of blades that were used in a day on that machine. That cut by two-thirds the $33,000 annual cost of blades. But that wasn't the only benefit.

From the saw, metal that has just been cut moves into a press machine, which uses heat as part of its operation. An even temperature must be maintained. "If the saw goes down for more than a few minutes, the press goes down as well," which means the press will cool and later must be reheated, Frye explains. By reducing downtime on the saw, "we saw an increase in press efficiency of 10 percent, and we also saw the quality of the metal go up (because a more even temperature is maintained)," he boasts.

Since some benefits cannot be predicted, how can a TPM advocate convince colleagues and managers that TPM should be implemented?

"I get in their face to start with," says Frye. "I let them know they're going to have to take some level of leap of faith. It's the right thing to do. Everybody wants this magic formula so they can figure out benefits to costs at the beginning. If managers aren't smart enough to see the kinds of benefits we'll get out of it, I don't want to work with them."

TAKEAWAYS

- TPM does not require major investments.
- Benefits from TPM come in many different areas.
- Not all benefits can be anticipated.

5

The Right Analysis Process Improves TPM Effectiveness

January, 2005

Total productive maintenance (TPM) becomes a more effective way of operating when it is accompanied by reliability centered maintenance (RCM).

That's the belief of managers at Whirlpool's dishwasher complex in Findlay, Ohio, where RCM — a process for analyzing equipment problems — was implemented in 2001, two years after a TPM initiative was launched.

"RCM is a tool that a TPM team can utilize to do more proactive work," says Richard Word, senior reliability engineer at the site. "It helps TPM to just do a better job." (See sidebar, page 27.)

Pairing the two approaches produces significant benefits, Word contends. Whirlpool regularly checks overall equipment effectiveness (OEE), the measure of a single piece of equipment's actual contribution as a percentage of its potential to add value to the value stream. "On average, we can increase the OEE about 10 percent (through RCM and TPM)," he declares. "I have seen it (increase) as high as 40 percent."

In addition, says Word, these kinds of improvement projects typically increase operator awareness of safety.

Another benefit is the awareness the operator gains of effective

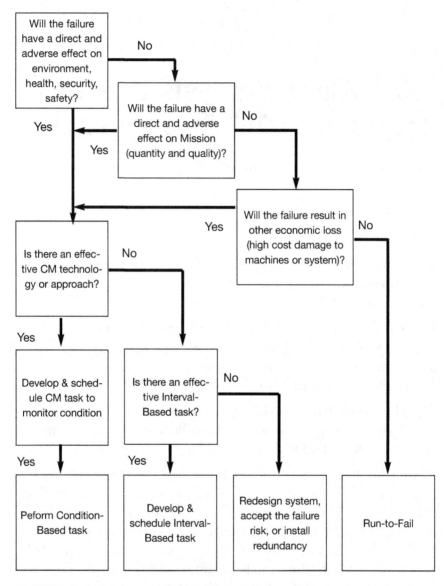

The RCM logic tree helps determine the best action for addressing equipment failures.

maintenance, through the sharing of information and ideas that occurs with cross-functional teams. "The operators, really after

What Is RCM

Reliability centered maintenance (RCM) is a process for determining and optimizing the maintenance activities for equipment or systems.

According to several sources, the heart of RCM is a series of seven questions that should be asked about the equipment or system. These are:

- What are the functions of the equipment?
- How can it fail?
- What causes it to fail?
- What happens when it fails?
- Does it matter if it fails?
- Can anything be done to predict or prevent the failure?
- What should be done if the failure cannot be predicted or prevented?

Determining the type of maintenance activity that should be planned for particular equipment involves navigating through an RCM decision logic tree (see diagram).

they get into it, start to understand the RCM process," Word notes. "They enjoy the process. It allows them to tell us about the chronic problems and issues — and solutions — they encounter every day."

Doing It Right

With more than 2,300 employees, more than a million square feet of manufacturing space, and more than half a million square feet of distribution space, Findlay claims to be the largest dishwasher manufacturing site in the world.

In its equipment-intensive operations, reliability of equipment is critical. The initial TPM effort was successful, Word recalls, but quickly regressed. Resistance to change was one factor; "when you are having operators do a lot of (maintenance) tasks without RCM, it is not so obvious why the operator should do it," he says. "We had experienced some resistance in the past."

Criteria for Choosing a System

A reliability centered maintenance program features criteria for selecting equipment or systems that will be the focus of improvement projects. According to the criteria, the system should be:

- A critical piece of equipment in need of an improved maintenance strategy.
- A system that immediately impacts production and/or has immediate negative economic consequences from poor reliability.
- A critical system that may be totally automated with no operator and is therefore not a good candidate for a TPM team.
- A system that has become a constraint for product flow.
- Equipment that recently encountered reliability problems.
- A system that will become much more reliable from ownership or operator awareness of the functions.
- A system that has a TPM team needing revitalization or several new members.

RCM was launched in the spring of 2000 with help from consulting firm Reliability Solutions. Whirlpool's stated goal for its new RCM process was to "apply a structured thought process to the expertise of a cross-functional team." More simply, the goal is "performing the right maintenance task, at the right time, by the right group and having the right part available."

The RCM process is aimed at identifying improvement opportunities, then analyzing those opportunities so that TPM can be applied in an ongoing way. The RCM analysis includes a set of criteria for identifying systems or equipment that provide the greatest opportunities for improvement (see sidebar above).

Once equipment has been identified as an improvement target, a detailed series of steps is followed to analyze its operation and determine how to improve it.

One example Word cites was Whirlpool's application of RCM to a machine that packaged manuals and instructions for dishwashers into plastic bags. "There's one (bag) for every unit we put out the door," Word notes. "That machine would not function with certain combinations, but it would run with other combinations. The people running the machine would say 'hey, we've got a problem.' The maintenance people would come over and, because the problem was so intermittent, the guy would say, 'well, it's running now.'"

An RCM analysis helped team members realize that, first, the time involved in the seemingly minor stoppages of the machine added up to a significant problem and, second, the source of the problem was a worn part that was previously ignored. "It was assumed that a crack in this part had no effect, but it did," says Word. A maintenance procedure was set up so that, in the future, the part would be checked regularly for wear.

More generally, he comments, the purpose of going through the RCM logic tree "is to direct us to what type of task can be done to either predict the failure, prevent the failure, eliminate the failure or determine a consequence reduction for that failure. And a minimum consequence reduction may be just to stock the part, if you can't predict, prevent or eliminate the failure."

In It for the Long Run

When Findlay first began its new maintenance processes, about 80 percent of all routine maintenance work was done by maintenance personnel and about 20 percent by equipment operators, Word estimates. As the program has matured, he says, those numbers have been reversed.

For the maintenance personnel, "because we can actually make processes more reliable with a more focused strategy, they can focus themselves on more efforts toward catching failures before they become breakdowns," Word notes.

Today, Findlay has 34 TPM teams, a figure that Word suggests may grow to about 50.

The key to success of an RCM/TPM program, he adds, is to "make sure that you really know what it is for the long run. People should really understand what (goals) are and what they should be. Be prepared. Do a reality check on how prepared you are to do it, how willing you are to be persistent in doing it.

"You want to make sure you have people who know they have to be participants, and not just spectators — and who want to be participants."

TAKEAWAYS

- Using RCM to identify maintenance needs strengthens a TPM program.
- The process must be well-defined, and the steps must be followed precisely.
- Everyone must understand the process and its goals.

6

You Can't Just Ignore Maintenance-Free Parts

September, 2003

A maintenance-free machine part isn't really maintenance-free; it's simply a part you can't maintain directly.

But you can take indirect actions to care for that part. By doing so, you make the part last longer — and you make it possible to accurately predict how long it will last.

That's the approach of Jim Leflar, productivity program manager for Agilent Technologies in Fort Collins, Colo. Leflar, who described Agilent's efforts at Productivity's 2003 TPM Conference, explains that the focus on maintenance-free parts grew out of a total productive maintenance program the company launched in 1997.

The overall goal "is to prevent machine failure through correct maintenance activities," says Leflar. "We measure the results by how much of our maintenance activity that we do is repair and how much is preventive maintenance. World-class is our goal; we consider world-class to be spending 90 percent of our time doing preventive maintenance and only 10 percent repair."

Agilent is a global, $6 billion company that was spun off from Hewlett-Packard in 1999. It makes a wide range of semiconductor, electronic and chemical products for industries that include communications, electronics, life sciences and chemical analysis. The

Light Bulb Shines for Maintenance Ideas

Agilent applied its principles of maintaining maintenance-free parts — involving looking at the part's inputs and outputs — to a light bulb.

Not just any light bulb. This bulb (shown below) is part of a Nikon Stepper machine (shown below), a $5 million piece of equipment that etches circuits on silicon wafers.

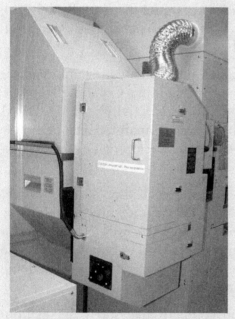

Replacing the bulb costs $1,600. The problem was that, when the bulb failed, it did so by exploding, causing $25,000 worth of damage inside the machine. The challenge was to maintain the bulb's environment so that technicians could reliably predict how long the bulb would last, and replace it before failure occurred.

The sole input to the light bulb is electricity. The company found it could maintain a precise voltage to the bulb, and eliminate voltage spikes, through a special power supply (shown at top of next page).

The bulb's outputs are light and heat. Heat is controlled through a cooling circuit.

Other possible issues, such as contamination and vibration, were determined not to be problems.

The maintenance routines established for the bulb include maintaining its cooling fan (shown below) by cleaning its filter, tightening hardware, lubricating moving parts and inspecting for minor abnormalities; and maintaining the environment of the electrical power supply by keeping it clean and

cool and regularly inspecting for minor abnormalities. The power supply is also regularly tested to ensure it is properly regulating the electricity.

All of this led to a determination that a properly maintained bulb could last 2400 hours. Therefore, the bulb is replaced after having been in use for that long.

Fort Collins plant makes computer chips used in a wide range of products. According to Leflar, the TPM program was initiated in Fort Collins and really hasn't spread to other plants, which "don't have our level of automated equipment and haven't shown much interest in TPM."

In 2001, Leflar explains, "we were trying to design maintenance to prevent parts from failing. The barrier was, people would look at a part and say 'there's nothing I can do to maintain it. It's a maintenance-free part.' Meanwhile, the part would keep failing. We said, 'no, you must prevent it from failing.' That's how the whole thing got started."

A sealed bearing is one example of a maintenance-free part; a light bulb is another. These are parts that cannot be opened, cleaned, lubricated or otherwise taken care of directly.

So, Leflar notes, Agilent developed a philosophy about these types of parts: "We really don't maintain the part. We maintain the world in which the part lives."

However, the philosophy by itself met with some skepticism. Leflar observes that "techs (maintenance technicians) don't like philosophies. They like specific instructions."

The approach Agilent takes is to look at a part's environment. With a sealed bearing, for example, "you want to make sure that you are not dripping water on it, that it's not in an overheated environment, you like it to run vibration-free. Vibration really takes out bearing life," Leflar says.

But the approach is really more organized than just looking at what is around a part. It's a process of identifying the inputs to, and outputs from, a maintenance-free part. One example is what Agilent did in reviewing light bulb failures in a machine that etches circuits on silicon wafers (see sidebar previous page).

"That's probably the real breakthrough here, the input-output environment," Leflar states. "We always tried to teach techs they had to maintain all parts. Then we ran into maintenance-free parts. We had to expand the thinking. We maintain the part by maintaining the world around it. That's easy to say, but when you get down to the nitty-gritty, it's 'what do you want me to do?'"

Another example occurred recently, Leflar says, when a pump that handles acid was failing frequently. "We found a leak in a valve on a suction line 15 feet away from the pump," he states. "It was sending air into the pump, causing premature failure. We've got to maintain the fittings on the suction line. The techs are beginning to connect that it's all part of the same system. Everything is connected."

Throughout its history, Agilent's TPM program — like most lean programs — has encountered barriers. The first one, Leflar recalls, was "overcoming the disbelief that minor defects are important. We finally convinced everybody. The way you convince them is you demonstrate it. You form pilot teams. You take a new step like that, and you take the nastiest machine in the plant. You try to convince people that if you can do it on this nasty machine, you can do it anywhere. You fix all the minor defects, and the machine would run much better. People would say, 'maybe you're right.'"

Agilent is proud of moving its maintenance efforts toward world-class, significantly decreasing the percentage of time spent on repairs. The company has not translated that achievement into dollars and cents; it has no figures on the financial impact. However, as Leflar sees it, it's just a matter of good sense.

"We regard it as obvious," he declares. "We have about a quarter-million dollars worth of machines. Good machines make many good products. Poorly running machines make few. Broken-down machines make none. Machines that work poorly just don't cut it. We're making very complex products. Machines make it. All the people do is service the needs of the machine. If the factory is full of machines that run well, we will crank out lots of good product. We consider that good business."

TAKEAWAYS

- Maintenance-free parts require maintenance of their environments.
- The inputs and outputs of such parts must be identified and maintained.
- Workers must be convinced that fixing minor defects is important.

7

A Day in the Park Becomes More Enjoyable Through 5S

July, 2005

Even an organization that doesn't create products or process transactions can benefit from implementing 5S and autonomous maintenance.

A parks department is not a manufacturer, and much of what its employees do is not manufacturing or office work. But top officials at Metroparks of the Toledo Area, a governmental subdivision in Ohio, are finding that lean techniques apply to their operations as well as anywhere else.

However, getting workers to believe that was not easy. Many office workers and field staff opposed the effort at the outset. It was only after a reorganization and a shift in strategy — including having employees rather than managers lead the effort — that the initiatives finally got moving.

"It's beginning to be part of the culture," says Rob Reimund, a district supervisor, "even though we are all at different levels. Some people are way ahead of others."

Funded by tax levies, grants and donations, Metroparks operates 11 parks and 2 trails spread across 8,600 acres in 4 counties.

The institution's 160 employees include about 10 full-time maintenance workers, with an additional 60 to 70 seasonal employees

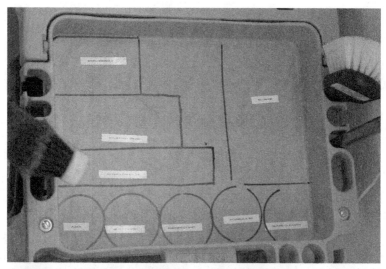

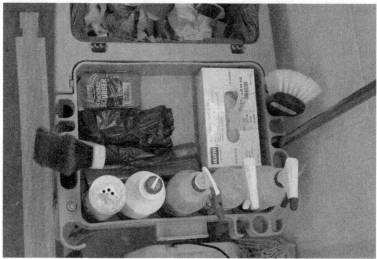

Techniques as simple as marking the exact location of cleaning supplies within a cart were used by Toledo Metroparks to improve the cleaning of restrooms.

who help maintain the parks during the summer months. There are also supervisors, support staff, marketing people and about 20 employees in the ranger department, which handles security.

There is always pressure to operate efficiently. "We want to better serve the public and be more conscious of our spending," says Reimund. "We run off of a tax base. The more we can prove to our constituents that we are being mindful of their money, the more likely they are to vote for (funding for) us."

Saving Time

Metroparks' first introduction to lean ideas came when the agency acquired a new director who had implemented 5S at a park district in Texas. In 2002, he started sending teams for training in 5S (for application in both maintenance operations and offices) and in autonomous maintenance (for equipment used by employees).

Not much happened for about a year, at least partly because of opposition from the office and field staff. But then a reorganization improved the prospects for implementation.

Managers got behind the initiative. More importantly, managers also stepped back, making sure the improvement efforts were employee-led — and they made sure the teams had the resources they needed to get the job done.

The primary focus of the 5S efforts so far has been not out in the parks, but in internal facilities — offices, storage closets, supply areas, and so on. Reimund says many of these were cluttered and dirty, and even unsafe. But now, with changes produced through 5S implementation, "when I go to the office to pick up supplies, I don't spend a lot of time looking for them," he states. "I get into the office and get out."

One particular example cited by managers involved applying 5S to a restroom facility, to make cleaning the restroom easier. The steps taken included putting storage racks and labels in place. The result was that cleaning the restroom after 5S took 10 minutes less than cleaning an identical restroom without having implemented 5S. The cleaning process for the two facilities involved the same procedures, products and supplies.

Ten minutes may not sound like much, but with nine identical facilities, the improvements save 90 minutes per day. Based on the fact that the restrooms never close and park labor costs $17 per hour, applying 5S to all restrooms saves more than $9,300 per year.

The total cost of improving the restrooms, including labor and a small amount spent on supplies (such as tape and a labeler) was $1,460.

More to Be Done

Metroparks is in the early stages of adopting autonomous maintenance procedures for its equipment. So far, that effort involves creating checklists for employees who use lawn mowers and other equipment, as well as for vehicles that may be used by different employees. The checklists are kept in the same location as the mowers, visible to anyone who goes to use one. Reimund notes that, since Metroparks hires many new seasonal employees each year, having clear instructions for the mowers can help reduce problems and damage.

The agency is also pursuing plans to install its first computer system to track maintenance activity, which officials hope will make problems more visible and identify where improvement efforts should be directed.

Reimund's advice to others pursuing 5S is to "have good reasoning be-hind why you are doing what you are doing, why you are focusing on this building or that equipment."

He adds, "The most important thing that I've found — the hard way — is that we need to start small. Even though every training I've been to suggests that, you get so excited that you want to do everything. That's not realistic. You set yourself up for failure."

TAKEAWAYS

- Empowering employees is critical to the success of an initiative.
- A measurable benefit of 5S is the time saved in performing tasks.
- Autonomous maintenance checklists can be particularly important when machinery is used by many people.

Part II
Managing the Initiative

OVERVIEW

TPM requires a change in outlook and approach by both operators and maintenance staff, with new attitudes regarding who does what when it comes to optimizing performance of equipment. Getting people to change the way they think and act – permanently – is the topic explored by the chapters in this section.

One of the first lessons learned is that it is easy to start off on the wrong foot. Chapter 8 describes how Kaiser Aluminum had a less-than-successful beginning to its TPM efforts by trying to do too much too soon. But the company learned from its mistakes and now has a better-structured and more successful initiative.

Building buy-in and support are critical to achieving the culture change necessary for a successful TPM initiative. Autoliv, Eastman Chemical, Motorola and Amoco Chemicals, the companies profiled in Chapter 9, all dealt with the challenges involved in creating TPM support.

Infrastructure is one of the keys to TPM success. The strategy at Intel, described in Chapter 10, involves creation of teams at several levels, with those teams involved in setting goals, developing strategy and implementing improvements.

Chapter 11 sets forth the philosophy at CME, where executives believe that 80 percent of management responsibility for TPM involves employee education. Helping employees understand what TPM is all about at the outset, while also employing key metrics such as OEE, are key to CME's strategy.

ON Semiconductor, profiled in Chapter 12, is another company that stumbled at the outset. This chapter explains what managers did wrong, how they recovered from their missteps and then stayed the course to achieve success.

Executives from a variety of manufacturers on a conference panel shared their insights into bringing about the paradigm shift required by TPM initiatives, a valuable discussion reported in Chapter 13.

At Parker Abex, top managers had to deal with a variety of issues – union concerns, employee training, old machinery and a new computer system – to achieve their TPM goals. Learn how they did it in Chapter 14.

And Chapter 15 discusses the challenges involved in sustaining a TPM strategy over time. Read about Kodak's commitment to its goals, and its strategy of constantly publicizing TPM activities and achievements during the several years it takes to create a TPM culture.

8

Kaiser Does TPM Wrong, Then Gets It Right

June, 2004

Executives at the two Kaiser Aluminum plants in Sherman, Texas, know how to do total productive maintenance right – because they started out doing it wrong.

By their own account, the company went too far, too fast. In their first attempt to implement TPM in 1999, they tried to address all maintenance issues everywhere without the proper support structure and without giving workers the time necessary to solve the problems.

"We went a mile wide and foot deep," says Rick Hartman, general manager. "We forgot things. We took on too much at one time."

The situation is different today. The plants now have a TPM coordinator. Maintenance issues are addressed in order of priority, not all at once. Operators are given clearer instruction on how to solve problems, rather than just on how to identify them.

Hartman believes that the initial problems occurred not only because of the structure of the TPM program, but because TPM was not attempted until after other lean initiatives had been launched.

The Sherman facilities – which are involved in the extrusion and fabrication of aluminum, and are, therefore heavily dependent on machinery – began a lean transformation in 1998.

"That's probably where we made our mistake," Hartman believes. "We jumped in and got all the low-hanging fruit. We should have done TPM first. We went from 18 million pounds of inventory to 3.5 million. Once you get down to those low levels, when something goes wrong, it's not long before a customer doesn't get something."

Changing Strategies

Kaiser first began TPM efforts in February of 2001, and had the program – as it existed at that time – fully deployed by the third quarter of that year.

Teams were educated on TPM, autonomous maintenance procedures were set up, and a variety of planning and training took place.

But by January 2002, the facilities were buried under what executives called a "green snow storm." Procedures had been established for attaching green tags to equipment needing maintenance. Managers had underestimated the amount of work that was needed, and more than 300 green tags were written, creating a maintenance order backlog.

In addition, the autonomous maintenance efforts were really not autonomous maintenance; they consisted primarily of inspections – people marking checklists – the results of which were written down and handed in, creating "a lot of data someone then had to go through," Hartman notes. Also, maintenance technicians were conducting those inspections, which executives subsequently realized was not the best use of the technicians' time or skills. Moreover, there was no system for setting maintenance priorities.

A new approach began in September 2003. The first step was creation of a management structure to support TPM, including a steering committee and designation of John Fitzmartin as the facilities' first TPM coordinator and continuous improvement manager. Hartman and Fitzmartin described their experience at Productivity, Inc.'s 2002 TPM conference in New Orleans.

Another significant development has been the implementation of new computerized maintenance management software (CMMS), which enables executives to manage and analyze the vast quantities of data generated by a TPM program. Inventory is bar-coded, so information on its status can be immediately scanned into the system.

Operators now have checklists that more specifically detail what they are looking for, and they have received training on how to fix some problems. They have the authority to stop the line to solve a problem, and only prepare a work order for someone else if they can't solve it. "The new system is more action-oriented," Hartman boasts.

Work orders are prioritized through Pareto analysis, and the most significant problems are addressed first. Overall equipment effectiveness (OEE) is used as a metric to help evaluate problems.

Benefits and Lessons

The new approach is producing benefits. For example, one improvement event addressed problems with a saw machine. In the past, the machine typically went through three blades a day, at an annual cost of nearly $33,000. After improvements in maintenance processes, the machine now consumes only one blade per day, reducing the cost by two-thirds. "Our production has really jumped up. We're getting more pounds per each blade," says Hartman.

In their presentation, Hartman and Fitzmartin listed what they see as the key lessons learned from their experience:

- Support structure is essential, and full implementation of TPM may take three to five years.

- TPM is not an event; it's a culture.

- Have a clear direction.

- Measure results.

- Never give up.

TAKEAWAYS

- TPM efforts must have the proper support structure in place, and workers must be properly trained.
- TPM implementation should not wait until after other lean initiatives are begun.
- A computer system may be necessary to handle the data generated from TPM efforts.

9

Implementers Offer TPM Tips

August 2000

Here are some tips and candid comments from speakers at Productivity, Inc. conferences and workshops about the challenges they face implementing TPM and how they are dealing with them.

It seems that every organization struggles with getting support from operators, maintenance techs, and senior management for the TPM effort. At Autoliv ASP's four facilities in northern Utah, TPM implementers made a concerted effort to win the backing of all these factions, beginning with senior management of the facilities in 1996.

Before that, some of the Utah plants had implemented elements of TPM on a limited basis with limited success. "It was getting very frustrating," said Gary Beadles, TPM trainer/facilitator. "We said, OK let's make a presentation to management and either do it or don't do it." This is how they made the case for TPM to management:

They gave a brief description of TPM, emphasizing what it could do for the Sweden-based company that makes seatbelts, air bags, and safety sensors for automakers. "By maintaining our equipment and making sure it runs as best as possible we ensure that we are making good quality parts for our customers," said Charlene Graham, TPM Coordinator. That's means air bags going off to save lives.

The presentation suggested calling the effort total productive manufacturing instead of total productive maintenance, so people couldn't dismiss it "as a maintenance department thing," recalled

Beadles. The new name helped position the effort as an approach to equipment management carried out by all employees through small group activities to prevent quality defects and unscheduled downtime.

"It was important that management understood that TPM would be a great tool to get those under control," Beadles explained. During the presentation, management learned that the six big equipment losses "dig right into the time we should be spending building good parts."

JIT Commitment

The presenters reminded management that preventive maintenance (PM) activities such as cleaning, inspecting, adjusting, and improvement activities, which would be emphasized under TPM, were customer driven. During plant visits, customers wanted to see records of PMs. And TPM would help the company achieve its JIT commitment to customers by helping to eliminate sporadic equipment failures.

The presentation also noted TPM's team-building element. For instance, it brings together people from all departments concerned with equipment and it requires the support and cooperation of everyone from top managers down. "We said TPM was a philosophy not a program and we needed their commitment to make it work," Beadles said.

Managers got a taste of what commitment would be needed. They attended an abbreviated autonomous maintenance workshop. "We didn't want them to come back later and say we didn't know what we were committing to," said Monte Carroll, TPM trainer/facilitator. "We basically got all the supervisors, managers, and plant managers into a two-day workshop consisting of time in the classroom learning about TPM and time on the shop floor cleaning and inspecting equipment to find abnormalities."

Presenters explained that machines or a production line would be down for four days during the regular workshop. "So they were going to lose some production" during the workshop and would have to schedule overtime or weekend shifts to fulfill JIT commitments to auto industry customers, he said.

TPM also would require team meetings, plus money for training and rewards such as hats and T-shirts, recognition dinners, and white boards in each area so teams could post information about what they had done. The boards would become a focal point of the conversion. "In our plant, management comes around and visits each cell and people gather around the board and talk about what they were doing, the improvements they are trying to get, and what the constraints are," explained Carroll.

Presenters also told management that the work cells would need the power to make some decisions to implement the changes they wanted to make.

Convincing management was one-third of the battle. When management approved the TPM implementation, operators and maintenance techs had to be convinced.

When the rollout began, maintenance techs complained, "What are you trying to do? You tell operators how to do this and I'll be out of a job," recalled Shane Misrasi, TPM trainer/facilitator. On the other hand, operators reacted to performing routine and preventive maintenance duties by saying, "What are you trying to do?" Turn us into maintenance guys? It's not our job."

Finding the "Border"

Autoliv responded by providing all maintenance and production personnel with basic TPM overview training. A four-day autonomous maintenance (AM) workshop followed. Since 1997, over 3,000 people from the four facilities have had the AM workshop. They discovered 8,668 abnormalities during the workshops and corrected 7,425 of them. Of the 1,243 work orders turned in to maintenance, more than 1,200 have been corrected so far. The outstanding ones require help from engineering.

The training is just one form of support. Each month, a TPM article appears in the plants' newsletters. And participation in the TPM effort became part of the annual employee review process.

To counter the feeling by maintenance techs that they were losing control of equipment, Autoliv asked them to write guidelines about what operators could and could not do to machines, and about safety procedures. A poll established how much operators knew about machine maintenance. The techs trained operators in the routine duties and "quick fixes" they could perform. Soon maintenance personnel realized they were responding to fewer "nuisance calls," said Misrasi.

That became a big benefit for maintenance personnel. Fewer nuisance calls meant they had time to work on more technical problems and fix fundamental problems. And operators liked having more production time by being able to correct minor problems quickly. "You have to find that borderline of what you can train associates to do and what you cannot do," said Misrasi.

Cristy Sneddon, TPM Trainer/Facilitator, compared TPM and sound medical practice when explaining TPM to associates. She likened it to a doctor seeing a heart patient on a regular basis for a checkup, and at each visit teaching the patient about her heart. "Do you think that would help her take better care of herself?" she asked. "But that doesn't mean she can go and performe triple bypass surgery.

"We're not trying to turn our associates into maintenance technicians, we're trying to get them to be the eyes and ears of maintenance. The more they know about their equipment, the better they are able to run it. The more small problems they can adjust and fix themselves, the less stressful their jobs are going to be and the more uptime they are going to have on their machinery."

Linked to Bonus System

Eastman Chemical Company had the support of several key managers when the Kingsport, Tenn.-based company began the effort in the late 1980s, recalled Michael McCloud, TPM coordinator at the Tennessee Eastman Division. A global chemical manufacturing company making plastics, chemicals, and fibers, the company's main Kingston plant employs about 8,000 people spread out among 400 production buildings on a site a mile long and almost a mile wide.

The company adopted TPM while looking for an improved approach to asset management during a period of rapid expansion in the 1980s. It saw TPM as a way of keeping craft-level employment constant. "We began looking at TPM because of the operator-based maintenance," said McCloud. "We felt it was something that would help us."

With operations helping to perform routine maintenance, the company could use the saved maintenance labor to introduce predictive technologies for improving equipment effectiveness. "We saw this not as a maintenance program but as a partnership between maintenance and operations groups," he said. In 1987, Eastman Chemical began three TPM pilot projects.

The company directed a lot of initial training at managers, explaining TPM theory, goals, and methodology. It used a lot of case studies to show what other companies had achieved with TPM, although most of the material in the late 1980s came from Japan. The training also included the OEE calculation to show what the plant's potential production rates were compared to what it was running currently.

To allay the job-loss fears of maintenance personnel, management issued a policy statement declaring that no one would lose a job because of any gains from the TPM activity.

Operators were more concerned that the PM duties would give them more work to do, but not more pay. Management issued a policy statement saying that it didn't expect TPM to affect jobs to an appreciable extent, but would perform a job study for operators who felt they were being affected. Two operators requested job studies and received pay increases.

The TPM effort was linked to the company reward system. Employees have 5 percent of their pay at risk, but each can draw an annual bonus of up to 30 percent of their base salary based on reaching return-on-assets goals. "Since we started this, we had one maximum payout of 30 percent. That was really nice," McCloud said. Most bonuses are in the area of 10 to 15 percent. The company estimates TPM has given it 300,000 hours of additional equipment availability per year.

Associates in Videos

To introduce employees to TPM theory and the reasons for implementing it, the company produced training videos with operators and maintenance techs for airing over the plant's television system. Before implementation began in a plant area, people received more in-depth training in TPM and the implementation process. These sessions also gave trainers the chance to meet face-to-face with people and answer their concerns.

By 1996, Eastman Chemical had established autonomous maintenance in nearly all manufacturing areas and was using predictive technologies bought with the savings from the TPM effort. To extend the TPM effort beyond the AM "pillar," the company formed a reliability technology department to assist manufacturing divisions in improving the reliability of equipment and processes by identifying, analyzing, and eliminating the root causes of losses. The company uses a number of reliability technologies, including computerized instrument calibration, vibration monitoring, ultrasonic testing, infrared thermography, and oil analysis.

Electrical Training

During these early efforts, implementation teams consistently identified two tasks for attention – de-energizing equipment to perform maintenance, and resetting motor starter overloads. Both tasks were extremely important to maintaining production flow. However, allowing nonelectrical personnel to perform electrical tasks represented a significant cultural change, noted McCloud.

Japanese TPM efforts had avoided electrical tasks, and many Eastman managers were concerned that a trainee might be injured, or that providing such training might increase the company's legal liability, he noted.

The company addressed these concerns by getting shop-floor electrical personnel involved in the development and delivery of the training. Senior level managers determined the criteria and limitations to be placed on the training. Training began in these tasks in March 1992.

Evaluation of available data proved electrical task training to be extremely beneficial, McCloud said. Requests to de-energize, re-energize, and reset electrical equipment were reduced by 20,000 calls per year, resulting in a maintenance labor cost savings of $1.2 million per year, he said. Annual equipment uptime gains in excess of 36,000 hours were realized.

The reduction of calls also contributed to reduced maintenance response times. Prior to training, the average response time for shift electricians was 54 minutes. Due to a decreased workload, response time was reduced to 18 minutes.

Surveys indicated the training was viewed positively. Only 3 percent of respondents reported they felt uncomfortable performing the electrical tasks. No accidents were reported during this time. In addition, allowing operators and mechanics to lock and tag out electrical equipment quickly led to increased interest in cross-training between crafts.

Since 1990, TPM has gradually become a part of the way Eastman Chemical does business. Maintenance courses are included in the company's operator apprentice program. General mechanic apprentices receive 148 hours of electrical classroom training, and electrical tech apprentices receive training in mechanical tasks such as pipefitting and rigging.

Starting Over

TPM had a tougher time becoming part of the business at the Sector Materials Organization (SMO) of Motorola, a unit of the company's Semiconductor Product Sector. TPM Manager Lisa Custer recalled that an implementation effort began in 1995 at the operator level. "We realized after not seeing the results we wanted that it was probably not the place to start."

The TPM steering committee began benchmarking TPM companies, bringing along maintenance supervisors, production supervisors, engineering managers for plant visits. In August 1998, the plant re-launched the TPM effort as total productive manufacturing, using "manager model teams" to teach TPM to the rest of the organization. At about the same time, the plant received word that it would be closed in about a year due to a business downturn.

The Phoenix-based SMO unit took raw polysilicon, grew crystal ingots from it at 1,400 degrees Celsius, sliced the ingots into wafers, polished the wafers, and applied a chemical layer to the wafers before selling them to internal customers. Just prior to its closure, SMO produced about forty-five percent of all the wafers used in Motorola wafer fabrication facilities. The plant began making wafers in 1958 and had the equipment to prove it.

Despite the looming closure, the implementation proceeded. The company saw the effort as a way of improving quality levels and keeping people focused on high standards during the shutdown. It also had an unanticipated effect.

"Everyone's job was going to go away," said Maria Purchine, TPM coordinator. So the usual maintenance concern over losing jobs became irrelevant. In fact, learning TPM was considered a valuable skill to have in landing jobs with other Motorola units or with other companies. Employees wanted to be "saleable," she said. "We were going to be skilled personnel who had a special edge. We were going to be the first ones who were hired, and that is what came about." Despite the impending shutdown, the effort produced effective ways of building involvement:

- The Adopt-A-Tool project in the crystal growing area let each operator "adopt" a piece of equipment. Purchine explained. After adoption, operators cleaned and tagged equipment to request repair of the five most important problems. Response to the program was overwhelming; approximately 75 percent of the equipment in the area was adopted. Prizes were awarded monthly, then quarterly, for the cleanest machine. Prizes ranged from movie tickets to watches, sweatshirts, and entertainment coupons. The program reduced scrap by over 60 percent and also cut equipment downtime.

- A newsletter promoted the TPM effort, informed people about TPM activities, and created a sense of fun about the effort. "It's one of the most marvelous forms of recognition to have your name in print," Purchine said.

- Area teams used activity boards to display their accomplishments, share one-point lessons, document TPM activities, present case studies, and any other information they felt good about. Cleanroom teams kept two boards, one inside their area and one outside the area so the team's information could be shared with others.

- An electronic Five-Why System ensured completion of a five-why questionnaire for each equipment failure. The system did not allow an operator to log equipment down without first filling out the appropriate portions of a five-why analysis. "An operator could not get that equipment back up again until the analysis was completed," said Purchine. The analysis needed the involvement of a maintenance tech to create partnership. The analysis required them to do such tasks as obtain information, determine if the problem was chronic, and how it could be prevented. They had to brainstorm together to find a corrective action. Everyone had access to the five-why printouts to share knowledge. Although some of the analyses were poor at the start, they improved "tremendously," she said. People included them with their resumes when applying for jobs.

Training Aid

To prepare for the plant closing, the company hired temporary employees as SMO employees found new jobs. There were nearly as many temps as regular workers just prior to closing. The TPM effort helped train the temps to run the equipment efficiently, said Betty Vanderlin, senior operations manager. She said most of the plant metrics were maintained or continued to improve, even while 65 percent of workforce was temporary. Ultimately all 650 regular employees found jobs with other company units or other companies, she said.

When the operation shut down, scrap was at 8 percent of value added, the lowest in plant history. Considered a breakeven operation supplying other Motorola units, SMO was making a profit at closure as a result of the TPM activities, Vanderlin noted.

Other results included a 65 percent improvement in customer complaints from 1996 to 1999. The cost of producing 1,000 square inches of silicon improved 57 percent during the same period, she said.

"We used less maintenance parts, we used less supplies, and the equipment was in better shape than in 30 years," Purchine said. She put the ROI on the TPM project at "about 120 to 1," pegging the entire cost of the effort at $150,000 for training, traveling for plant visits, and training supplies."

Spreading Success Sitewide

Amoco Chemicals recorded positive results from implementing TPM among its 12 chemical and 3 fabric-producing sites between 1997 and 1999. The sites, 3 of which were overseas, ranged in size from $300 million in assets to $2 billion. But most of the successes were at the department level. Management wanted to spread the effort sitewide, said Mark Lawrence, a maintenance and reliability internal consultant for the new Houston, Texas-based BP Amoco Chemicals.

So, the TPM steering committee asked the individual plants to really understand their culture and people issues. Sites varied from unionized ones in the North to nonunion in the South with diverse cultures and people issues. "That was the main thing we wanted from the sites," said Lawrence. "Look at your site. Look at your people. Where can you get an early success?"

The steering committee wanted the plants to pick one of five areas to start sitewide implementation:

1. Establish equipment improvement teams

2. Maintenance effectiveness

3. Early equipment management

4. Reliability engineering

5. Autonomous maintenance

Don't Wait for Buy-In

"Of those five, which one would you work on first? Where have you had success in the past?" said Lawrence, explaining the questions facing plant management, which had to demonstrate support and monitor results.

Right away "a couple of union sites went ballistic" because they had "bad information" about TPM, he recalled. The company developed a two-to-three day "TPM 101 course" to spread accurate information and develop implementation teams.

Despite the opposition, the effort was pushed forward. "If you wait until you have complete buy-in and completely understand TPM before you start, you'll never get started," Lawrence said. He noted there are four areas where you can begin a TPM implementation and make progress while people learn:

1. Condition monitoring. The company gave operators elec-

tronic data collection tools and created condition monitoring routes for them. Operators began taking temperatures, pressures, and trending the data to begin identifying problems before they happened.

2. Work Order prioritization. Identify the most important jobs and do them first.

3. Equipment improvement teams. Start training them in problem-solving tools, give them time and problems to solve.

4. Clean to inspect. This is AM by operators.

"Do these four things while you're figuring out the rest of your plan," said Lawrence. "This way you can get started right away instead of having a six-month lag."

He also advised that you leverage any plant that is already pursuing TPM successfully. Amoco had a plant that was two years into the effort. At the end of the TPM 101 classes, operators and maintenance techs from the plant joined site management for a panel discussion.

"Having an operator talk to an operator about the ways his job changed and have this operator say he would never ever go back doing things the way they used to" is invaluable, noted Lawrence. Just as important is having a maintenance tech say he was doing more technical tasks and condition monitoring, not just "changing the same old seals day after day or changing out parts."

TAKEAWAYS

- Convincing management of the value of TPM is critical and can only be achieved by making a solid case with a detailed explanation of what is involved.
- TPM should be a partnership between maintenance and operations, with both groups involved.
- Implementation should not begin at the operator level.

10

Focusing the TPM Effort

March, 2000

The nature of operations at Intel's Santa Clara, Calif., facility made it a natural candidate for a TPM implementation. As a year-round, 24 x 7 operation, equipment reliability is crucial. The chip-making equipment also needs an uninterrupted supply of electricity, water, steam, gases, chemicals, and waste-treatment services to remain online.

Every hour the chip-making equipment isn't making chips because of an unscheduled interruption costs77 hundreds of thousands of dollars in lost production. In addition, interruptions often damage wafers in process, turning them into scrap.

Planned downtime (PM) isn't cheap either. It costs tens of thousands of dollars per hour. The 7.6 million-square-foot facility has more than 7,500 pieces of equipment and spends more than 100,000 hours annually in PMs.

Given the impact of downtime in a market where microprocessors are quickly changing from a consumer product into a commodity item, remaining competitive demands minimizing – if not eliminating – interruptions to production and shortening the downtime of PMs.

Another natural link between Intel and TPM was the accord between TPM principals and the company's long-standing motto of "better, faster, cheaper," explained Scott Giles, facilities technician.

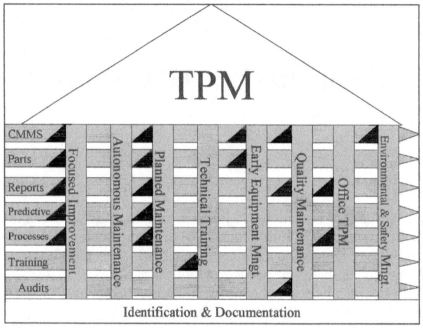

Source: Intel

The chart uses the eight TPM development activities or "pillars" to represent the architecture of the TPM effort at Intel, Santa Clara. The dark triangles where arrows meet pillars indicate the focus of a TPM subteam listed at the far left. The chart is also a practical device, indicating where more resources are needed such as in the areas of autonomous maintenance and auditing.

Despite the connection, the plant's early effort at TPM was a learning experience. The initial effort revealed obstacles to overcome, such as a lack of widespread knowledge about TPM goals, lack of an overall implementation plan, and lack of sufficient documentation and maintenance data. The computerized maintenance management system (CMMS) lacked the needed documentation and data about equipment, materials and parts, tools, and engineering. Such records would help create a common set of data that would serve as a foundation for implementing the eight TPM development pillars. (See sidebar, p. 62-63.)

Conserving Resources

To get the TPM ball rolling, the plant formed a Core Team to serve as a central coordinating and prioritizing body of TPM activity leaders, managers, and technical experts. This team focused the plant's TPM effort, eliminating redundant activity so numerous TPM activities could proceed without exhausting limited resources. The team also formulated a cohesive plan for success, which it defined as "increased reliability and enhanced efficiency."

The Core Team developed a business plan, a comprehensive document that defined a mission, responsibilities, goals, the team structure, a roadmap of TPM milestones, and indicators for progress to give people a common sense of direction.

The business plan document identified key team members who would be needed on the team and their specific roles. Team members are not dedicated solely to TPM activities.

The business plan also outlined a communication plan that described what points to cover when communicating progress back to the organization, among facilities, and among the subteams responsible for implementation. The plan also listed key objectives for the next quarter and how progress would be tracked.

"Much of this may seem like unnecessary formality," said Giles, "but we found it quite important to have all the points well defined to help teams stay on track and cover multiple initiatives."

Subteams

Small groups called subteams actually do the TPM activities aligned with the eight development pillars. (See chart opposite.) The efforts of the subteams complete the plant's TPM architecture, supported by a foundation documentation and identification.

The subteams, which meet periodically, concentrate on one or more of the following areas: the CMMS, predictive maintenance, materials and parts, standardizing how information is reported, process development & improvement, training, and auditing performance. "These teams promote and direct the activities focused on some or all of the pillars," Giles said.

TPM Development Activities

The following eight activities are the most common ones for implementing TPM effectively and efficiently. When properly implemented, they form the foundation that will support any successful TPM effort. Not all of these strategies are implemented at once. Each company will develop a sequence that fits its situation.

1. Focused improvement (kaizen) activities are performed by cross-functional teams composed of such people as production engineers, maintenance personnel, and operators. These activities are designed to minimize targeted losses that have been carefully measured and evaluated.

2. Autonomous maintenance activities, one of the

TPM

Focused Improvement | Autonomous Maintenance | Planned Maintenance | Technical Training | Early Equipment Mngt. | Quality Maintenance | Office TPM | Environmental & Safety Mngt.

8 Key Strategies of TPM Development

Following the Core Team format, each subteam created a business plan specific to its activities that delineated goals and listed members and their responsibilities. "It's important to remember that this is a living document that will be periodically reviewed by the team to be sure the plan meets current business needs," Giles explained.

Each team listed three significant objectives to achieve and how they will go after them. "They don't have to put together a huge list," said Giles, "just go after a couple of key objectives initially" and report back how they are doing.

The initial TPM strategy aimed to:

most distinctive features of TPM, involve operators in the routine maintenance and improvement of equipment.

3. Planned maintenance or scheduled maintenance includes breakdown, preventive, and predictive maintenance. Planned maintenance activities stress monitoring mean-times-between-failures data to specify the intervals between activities in annual, monthly, and weekly maintenance schedules.

4. Technical training in equipment maintenance and operation identifies the specific knowledge, skills, and management abilities people should have so the right training programs can be designed to instill them.

5. Early equipment management aims to have products that are easy to make and equipment that is easy to use. It addresses equipment and process design, fabrication, test, and startup management.

6. Quality maintenance activities build in quality by managing variability in a quality characteristic by controlling the condition of equipment components that affect it.

7. Office TPM means that administrative and support departments must supply high-quality and timely information for TPM activities and must streamline the flow of information.

8. Safety and environmental management includes implementing accident prevention training, near-miss analysis, and ways of preventing adverse environmental impacts.

- Reduce maintenance costs using predictive technology such as vibration analysis and ultrasound scanning to detect potential problems before they occurred and to avoid intrusive PMs, thus saving labor and material.

- Use the CMMS to standardize the techniques and procedures used during PMs to develop the best-known methods for the organization.

- Predict and, therefore, avoid system or process failure.

- In the event of a major system failure, minimize the impact through contingency planning.

Achievements so far include spreading TPM overview training throughout the organization. More concretely, cost savings of more than $400,000 in the past four quarters came from detecting problems before equipment failed and making process changes to eliminate redundant or ineffective maintenance.

Plans call for concentrating on strengthening the foundation of the TPM effort through training to build support for more improvement activities, improving equipment documentation, and coordinating the PM activities of various work centers to improve efficiency and minimize PM-related downtime. "This will allow more maintenance to be accomplished within the limited windows of opportunity we have for shutdown maintenance," Giles explained.

TAKEAWAYS

- Successful implementation requires widespread knowledge of goals, an overall implementation plan and sufficient documentation and maintenance data.
- A multi-level team structure can be an effective approach.
- A full range of activities is required to implement TPM, though not all are implemented at once.

11

Education, Support Drive TPM Success

June, 2002

The total productive maintenance program at the CME plant in Mt. Pleasant, Mich. has produced the kinds of benefits typical of such programs, including significant gains in overall equipment effectiveness (OEE).

Mike Gardner, who holds the title of lean leader at the plant, is proud of that achievement. But he places equal emphasis on how the TPM program has changed the attitudes of company employees.

"Before they became involved, people kind of had an attitude that they run machines and run parts. Now they're regularly taking some ownership in the equipment," he says. "There's a kind of attitude that 'yes, this is our company, and this equipment pays my salary, and I'm going to do what I can to learn about it and take care of it."

That's the type of change that might be praised by a teacher discussing his students. Indeed, Gardner says that about 80 percent of his work involves employee education. And it is education, he is quick to add, that has played a key role in the success of TPM at CME, an automotive supplier that makes motors for wiper systems, fans, starters, and power windows, among other products.

Part of what motivates Gardner and others at the plant — and val-

The TPM program at CME has raised overall equipment effectiveness from 55 percent to 91 percent.

idates their efforts — are the numbers. When TPM first got under way at the CME site in 1999, Gardner measured OEE at an average of about 55 percent.

(OEE is the primary metric of TPM. It indicates a single piece of equipment's actual contribution as a percentage of its potential to add value to the value stream. The calculation is: % availability x % standard run rate x % first pass quality.)

Gardner also determined that the average OEE of Mitsuba, CME's Japanese parent company, was about 84.5 percent.

Today, CME's number is at 91 percent. That figure translates into productivity improvements, cost savings and less downtime. The average improvement in a 12-month period is about 25 percent, Gardner says.

"When you put something down in a numerical format, it is so much easier to show the benefits to other people on the shop floor, and to the management," he observes.

Critical Success Factors

CME employs 300 people at the Mt. Pleasant facility. A sister plant is located in Monroeville, Ind., and offices for R&D and sales are in Ann Arbor, Mich. The company has annual revenues of about $240 million, up from only $35 million in 1989. (With Honda of America as its chief customer, CME has been virtually untouched by the recession.)

While CME had what Gardner calls a "small, informal preventive maintenance system" in its early years, people "kind of lost touch with it" during the rapid growth that included significant new equipment purchases.

Near the end of 1996, Gardner visited Mitsuba's operations in Japan and saw what the parent company was doing with a formal TPM program. He brought back ideas from that visit, bought books, attended conferences and studied TPM in depth, becoming something of a self-taught expert in the field. He pushed for a local program, but, by his own account, with limited success.

Then two events occurred that brought TPM to the forefront. Art Gase became manager of the Mt. Pleasant plant in 1998 and gave strong support to Gardner's TPM push. "He basically gave me a free hand to get if off the ground," Gardner states.

And in early 1999, the company decided to seek QS 9000 certification. Within that effort, "I picked up on predictive and preventive maintenance as a lever I could use" to move TPM forward, he notes.

From the beginning, the program enjoyed strong support from plant management, which Gardner says has been a critical success factor. Plant manager Gase "has not only been supportive, but he has been a driver and a leader," Gardner says. "He has taken ownership of one piece of equipment; he actually performs preventive maintenance on the floor. It sets a good example."

Education has been equally critical to the initiative, by "giving people the opportunity to learn what it's all about before you throw it at them," Gardner declares. Each associate goes through 18 hours of training, half in the classroom, half on the shop floor. Departments are certified based on the training of their employees.

Public recognition is the third key to success, Gardner says. The company has a "tree" on a wall; when a department is certified, it receives a leaf on the tree. Team members receive incentives that include inscribed gold-plated key chains and miniature flashlights, the gift determined by the level of certification. Accomplishments are also recognized publicly at monthly company meetings.

An Ongoing Process

TPM began at CME with a pilot project on one fully automated line that manufactured windshield wiper motor armatures. That operation began with an availability rate of 75 percent, Gardner says, a number that has since risen to 96 percent.

When the TPM program began, he adds, the company knew it had problems, not only because of the low OEE figure, but in the form of customer complaints and missed shipments. In a posting on the website of the Lean Enterprise Institute, he described the use of OEE in solving problems:

"I dug into the OEE and realized the initial reject rate was our biggest loss. We then began to address this. As time went on, we improved the initial reject rate immensely, but the OEE didn't climb very much. We then dug into the NEW biggest problem — machine downtime. We continued in this manner, using standard QC tools, SPC, why-why analysis, TPM and the rest of the normal tool box until we were able to eliminate each problem, all the while using OEE to tell us which area was our biggest problem and how solving each problem affected our overall effectiveness. Three years later, we are running well into world-class OEE, have a happy customer, and are making good profits from this product."

Beyond TPM, CME is actively pursuing a broad range of lean manufacturing initiatives. Managers known as section leaders are now called value stream leaders and are charged with implementing lean systems within each product family. They focus on creation of "supermarkets," inventory reduction, line flow, line balancing, moving equipment and creating cells, Gardner says, adding, "this really has become our manufacturing direction.

He notes that lean initiatives including creation of a supermarket pull system led to the discovery, in connection with a particular stamping press, "that instead of having to work overtime to meet demand, there was actually quite a bit of excess capacity. Now there is some planned downtime every week. That's kind of a positive spiral that enables them to meet demand."

Gardner is now focusing on equipment design. Mitsuba builds most of CME's equipment, and over the next 18 months, he says, he will be working with Mitsuba equipment designers to "design for reliability, and make it possible for us to perform basic TPM activities easier." This might include making sure that gauges are at eye level, or that lubrication points are easily accessible, for example.

Gardner is also expanding his educational offerings. The company will conduct a fundamental course for support departments, such as shipping and receiving, quality assurance, and the maintenance department, "so they can work with their own equipment better and get a better idea of what people on the manufacturing floor are up to," he explains.

TPM is an ongoing process, he stresses, and "not something you do overnight."

TAKEAWAYS

- Changing employee attitudes is just as important as changing maintenance procedures.
- Education is critical to changing employee attitudes.
- Public recognition of successes helps drive culture change.

12

Failures & Countermeasures Move TPM Effort Forward

June, 2005

In the real world, implementations of lean manufacturing and total productive maintenance (TPM) are never perfect. There are always failures and missteps. The challenge is to learn from your mistakes and make things better.

At ON Semiconductor's Zener Rectifier factory, located in Phoenix, things have gotten better. The plant, which was on the verge of closure a few years ago due to poor performance, has been turned around, with dramatic gains in all aspects of operations.

But plant executives are the first to say that the improvement effort, particularly in regard to TPM, did not start out well. Four TPM teams were formed in the summer of 2003, but success was limited. Managers attempted a revitalization of the effort late that year, slimming down to two teams and laying a foundation for improvement that had been missing earlier.

"We definitely had a false start," admits John Hall, operations manager. "We had put the cart before the horse." The company had created the teams without formalizing structure or overall strategy, and "we made the assumption that we had enough of a base of a skill set to skip that — and we didn't. We didn't have the infrastructure, the guidelines. We didn't know what we wanted to do."

He adds, "There is a curve to culture development, and there is a

Application of 5S and other lean tools at ON Semiconductor's Zener Rectifier factory in Phoenix helped transform one area that was cluttered, with supplies hard to locate (top), making it cleaner with wider aisles and materials that could be more easily located (bottom).

curve to continuous improvement and any kind of change management. We weren't ready for where we said we were. We skipped the appropriate steps."

Clarity and Structure

The solution — what Hall labels the "countermeasure" — was clear. A formalized structure was developed and an overall strategy devised. The two teams created during the TPM revitalization were focused on the grinding and aligner operations at the plant. The grind team, for example, was given clear direction as to what it was expected to deliver (eliminate grind as a factory bottleneck) and what its goals were (specific targeted improvements in downtime, running time, quality, and so on).

Management Failure

The failure to sustain teams due to a lack of structure and strategy was one of four early TPM failures, according to Hall, although all are related.

The second was inconsistent cross-team expectations and goals. Others were teams being reactive toward immediate factory issues, and cleanliness expectations varying across several areas and shifts, leading to deteriorating team standards.

"It was just kind of a failure to thrive. The meetings didn't have energy. You could see it in the faces of the people. The metrics weren't changing," says Hall.

He doesn't blame the teams: "It was a management failure. Management didn't scope it out. People wanted to do it. Upper management did not support it in the factory. That's me and my staff."

"We got back together and I said 'look, we are not going to fail at this,'" he adds. "We asked, 'what did we learn from this?' We had some very frank discussions."

Standard Expectations

With those discussions, and help from consultants, the plant got back on track. Ken Kozik, manufacturing manager, notes that with improvements to the grind operation, "we blew the grinders so far open that they became so not our problem. We were able to go work on other things."

The problem of inconsistent cross-team expectations meant that "we didn't have the same expectation for each team," Hall explains. "We hadn't standardized checklists. We expected more out of some teams than other teams, and that's not right. The goal is perfection. We came up with standard templates for presentations. You had to hit a minimum on our standard template. It became minimum gates for understanding OEE, tool cleanliness, autonomous maintenance. People did respond well to that because people started to understand their requirements better. Everyone, when they come to work, wants to do a good job. It's our job to show them how to channel their energies. By setting standards, we allowed people to understand their objectives better."

Hall says that when he describes teams as being reactive, he means they were not proactive enough. "An example might be where operators would load tools, and they knew that for the exact same device, they would take more time on one tool than another, but they wouldn't do anything about it," he comments. "Another thing, we would probably run tools that were slightly impaired. Now people are becoming more intent on putting the tool down if it isn't right."

What has helped turn that around is a greater demonstration of high-level sponsorship as well as steering group guidance.

Hall explains the variation in cleanliness expectations by saying, "Some people had accepted that 'I work in an area that grinds wafers. It's going to be dirty. Their area cleans wafers, it will be cleaner.' I went in and explained to them, no, it still has to be just as clean."

Of course, there was more to the solution than a simple explanation. The problem was also addressed by increased efforts on the factory-wide 5S initiative, which had preceded the TPM efforts (see sidebar opposite). "You get back to basic targets and objectives, the

Evolution, Not Quite According to Plan

The TPM efforts at ON Semiconductor's Phoenix Zener Rectifier plant are one stage of a five-stage continuous improvement evolution under way for several years. And that evolution has been shaped as much by market realities as by management planning.

Like many lean implementations, the journey began with 5S, which was followed by creation of TPM pilot teams.

The third stage was the development of lean manufacturing teams — although if the market situation had been different, the path might have been different.

Demand was high for the company's semiconductors, and "we needed to get more wafers out," says operations manager John Hall. "Business requirements allowed us the opportunity to add a tremendous amount of capacity," which was achieved by applying lean principles.

The fourth stage in the journey has been an attempt to integrate lean, TPM and six sigma efforts under an umbrella the company calls ZOOM — Zener Rectifier Organization Optimized Manufacturing.

Without the pressure to increase capacity, "lean and ZOOM would probably have been reversed," Hall comments.

Most recently, in the fifth stage of the evolution, the emphasis is on autonomous and planned maintenance (AM/PM). The purpose of that effort is to instill a culture based on equipment standards, ownership and cascading employee knowledge throughout the plant. Thirty-nine AM/PM teams have been formed to focus on 373 critical pieces of equipment, with plans to complete the initial steps of autonomous maintenance within a defined timeline.

rules of engagement, using resources correctly," says Hall. "You go back to 5S rigorously. You can always go back to 5S." Ongoing audits and clear standards of cleanliness are also essential.

Hall's advice to others involved in TPM efforts is straightforward: "Get some outside help. Understand what it is you are trying to do before you get started. Get some wise counsel from somebody who has done it before, and get your operators involved, at least from a dialogue standpoint, right from the start. You cannot over-communicate what you are trying to do."

TAKEAWAYS

- Structure and strategy are necessary before improvements begin.
- Expectations cannot vary from team to team.
- A lean journey may not take place as planned due to market conditions.

13

Soft Side Gets Hard Look

October, 2003

People issues, not equipment problems, were the challenges most on the minds of presenters and attendees at a conference on lean equipment.

The 11th Annual Total Productive Maintenance (TPM) Conference and Exposition, sponsored by Productivity, Inc. drew 453 people to Dallas during four days of implementation workshops, conference sessions, and product showcases.

Supporting the Effort

The Eight* TPM pillars are:
1. Focused Improvement
2. Autonomous Maintenance
3. Planned Maintenance
4. Training & Skill Development
5. Early Equipment & Product Management
6. Quality Maintenance
7. Administrative Systems
8. Environmental/Safety/Health Systems

* This list is the traditional five TPM pillars, plus Quality Maintenance, Administrative Systems, and Environmental/Safety/Health Systems.

Keynoter Michael Woolbert, quality team leader, Phillips Petroleum, said focusing on machines or the eight "pillars" of TPM is "not enough" to have a successful implementation (see box, Supporting the Effort).

"People are the focus and benefactors" of TPM and when they feel successful and respected they are motivated to participate in continuous improvement efforts, he said.

In response to a question from the audience, Woolbert warned about paying people incentives for participating in TPM activities. "If you want TPM to be something people do only when they get a cookie, give them an incentive," he said. "I'd be very careful with incentives." He said they could "trivialize" the improvement effort.

Preferably, people should believe in the TPM philosophy of zero breakdowns and zero defects and perform improvement activities because they are the right things to do for themselves and the company.

He said Phillips used a simple reward and recognition system built around giving people caps and t-shirts when they are cited by peers for doing the right things.

Woolbert also cautioned attendees, who represented both process and discrete industries, not to misunderstand the level of senior management support they need to have a successful effort. "If you have resources and a budget [for TPM], you have management support," he said.

More importantly, the change process needs leadership. Leaders:

- Inspire us to think he or she is in charge

- Create emotional connections between people and ideas

- Generate respect from the team

- Care about both people and the job

As examples, he cited the behaviors of well-known leaders such as General H. Norman Schwarzkopf during the Persian Gulf War, and legendary Notre Dame football coach Knute Rockne.

"We have tougher jobs" as TPM leaders because TPM leaders must advocate "smaller ideas" than winning a war or a big game, said Woolbert. These ideas will sound like nonsense to many people and will take at least three years to implement.

Thus, business leaders must:

- Inspire us to think he or she is in charge

- Create emotional connections between people and ideas
- Generate respect from the team
- Care about both people and the job, plus
- Sell novel ideas
- Stay focused for the long haul

To succeed, TPM leaders must be "part Arnold Swartzenegger, part Albert Einstein, and part Energizer Bunny." Mostly, they have to be part bunny. "You have to keep on keeping on," he said. "You must be tenacious to be a TPM leader. And the minute you stop thinking of yourself as a leader, you aren't."

Woolbert also said people misunderstand how to alter the culture while implementing a continuous improvement effort. Don't let resistance "tie you up," he advised. Cultural change will gradually follow the actions you take. "There are no knobs on culture" that allow for quick and easy adjustments, he said.

The big obstacle to change is inside people's heads – their paradigms or sets of accepted ideas. "Paradigms really are what we are up against as TPM implementers," said Woolbert.

Paradigms simplify the decision-making process for people and make them feel comfortable. "That's a key motivator for people – they want to feel comfortable."

Change attacks these "comfort systems" of managers and workers "so resistance is high," Woolbert said. As a result, the people leading the change effort aren't going to be liked by everybody. "Give up being liked," said Woolbert. "Go for respect. You can't run for prom queen forever."

One-Point Lessons

Attendees learned that an effective tool for changing people's paradigms is the one-point lesson, also known as a single-point lesson. (See Figure 1.) Joseph Beaulieu, manager, Stanley Production

| ONE-POINT LESSON | Dept.: _____ Date prepared: _____ |
| | Team: _____ Prepared by: _____ |

| The Role of FRLs-Lubricators | Type: Basic pneumatic device |

Why are lubricators necessary?
The lubricator works on the atomization principle. The oil mist produced prevents the interiors of pneumatic piping and equipment from rusting and helps pneumatic devices to operate smoothly by lubricating cylinder walls.

Drip-rate adjustment knob

Principles
- The surface of the oil inside the sight glass (A) remains constantly under the pressure of the air on the inlet side.
- When the pneumatic device actuates, the inlet-side pressure exceeds the outlet-side pressure. Oil is drawn up the suction pipe and forms a droplet (B).
- This droplet falls down and mixes with the incoming air (C).
- The oil is atomized and passes out with the outgoing air.

Air inlet
Air outlet
Suction pipe
Oil level control range
Sight glass
Filter

Drip-rate Adjustment
- Adjust the drip rate so that a drip is formed while the piston of the hydraulic device is still moving.
- If the oil drop forms after the piston has completed a full stroke, the cylinder walls will not be lubricated.
- Do not allow the oil level to fall below the suction pipe intake

Training Completed	Date:						
	Trainee:						
	Checked:						

Figure 1

System, The Stanley Works, and Rick Glasmann, high vacuum technology leader, International Rectifier (IR), both shared success stories about these brief visual aids. One-point lessons use one sheet of paper to succinctly address one issue or problem with text and graphics. They cover three types of information:

1. Basic knowledge about what people must know for everyday production or participation in improvement activities.

2. Key points for helping operators and technicians identify a problem, such as a breakdown or defect, and how to correct the problem.

3. Improvement case studies share the concepts and results of actual improvements made on the shop floor so similar

improvements can be made in other areas.

Glasmann said the keys to changing people's mindsets were asking for their ideas, respecting the idea, and implementing them in kaizen events and through one-point lessons. At his facility, which makes semiconductors, operators and technicians co-write lessons following a computerized template. Supervisors tell operators and technicians when a new lesson is issued.

At Stanley, operators tell their improvement ideas to the plant's Stanley Production System manager, who creates the photos and text on a standardized form. Beaulieu and six other Stanley Production System managers review each lesson that is submitted.

The completed lessons are displayed right at the appropriate machines. Lessons also are available through Stanley's intranet. To help the intranet manager properly file each lesson, each one is sorted into one of several categories. The intranet shows what lessons were submitted during the week, so each Stanley Production System manager can quickly see what is new and disseminate them.

Individuals or teams submitting lessons get Stanley clothing as rewards. Beaulieu shared examples of one-point lessons from plants:

- A large vibrating bowl fed small parts into a machine. Because it sat above the machine, it was difficult for operators to check the parts in the bowl for problems or potential problems. One plant installed a mirror so the operators could easily check the condition of the parts. "All of a sudden, we were buying mirrors like crazy," recalled Beaulieu. Other plants had quickly picked up the idea from the intranet.

- Another lesson shared information for preventing breakdowns on a CNC lathe. Dust in the lathe's motor fan led to the fan's failure and ultimately failure of the motor from overheating. New electric motors cost $15,000; rebuilt ones are $8,000. Fans were cleaned and filters installed.

Operators check the condition of the filter during daily preventive maintenance checks. However, a small piece of string was tied to the filter covers. If the string isn't moving, the operators know the fan has stopped and can shut down the machine and take corrective action before the motor overheats and fails.

Beaulieu said the point of the lessons was to "capture and share intellectual knowledge" of operators and technicians.

Training's Payback

The savings from avoiding breakdowns and emergency repairs will more than pay for the improved equipment management effort, said Rick Fox, training manager, LG&E Power Services, during a panel discussion on training. He estimated the company, which manages power plants, passed the breakeven point on its training investment after two-and-a-half years.

Alden Salcedo, training development consultant, International Rectifier, said the key in training is to target the investment at areas that will give you a significant return. He noted that besides attacking the obvious costs of breakdowns and defects, training also hits the hidden costs from absenteeism, low morale, and poor employee involvement.

In response to a question about why some companies "spin their wheels" when trying to implement TPM, Fox said many organizations concentrate on technical training, neglecting "soft" training in team skills. "You can't put five guys in a room and tell them, You are a team now. You've got to invest some money in soft skills, but that's what the bean counters have trouble with because it's intangible."

Fox said his company sends employees to train-the-trainer classes so they can deliver training to other workers. He estimated everyone spends four hours per week in training, besides time spent in kaizen events.

Salcedo said companies "spin their wheels" because the implementation effort is not linked to strategic initiatives. "Eighty percent of TPM implementation is planning," he said. "If you put the upfront investment in planning, training, and what you want out of it as a company" you are more likely to succeed.

Showing how TPM and lean supports the corporate strategy is "how you get senior management support," Fox added.

Another attendee asked if an implementation could succeed in a plant or area without the involvement of senior managers, who kept changing in his company due to acquisitions and mergers.

"Going from the bottom up is really not the way to do this," cautioned Fox. However, a bottom-up effort can work if the plant manager is very knowledgeable and very involved in the effort. "The plant manager and staff has to be involved," he said. The effort at LG&E began at the top.

And you must have measures in place so you can show "in black and white" how much money was saved in overtime, or downtime, or defects, etc. compared to other plants, Fox advised.

If you are a functional or area manager, "there's a lot you can do, but understand where your boundaries are," advised Salcedo.

Tom Jackson, president and CEO, Productivity, Inc., noted that companies don't hesitate to spend $200 million on a new transfer line, but hesitate to spend money to train people. "It goes into a different mental bucket and prevents us from thinking about people as part of technology," he said.

During a keynote address, Jackson said the future of TPM "depends on the attention span of business leaders." Continuous improvement requires a long-term commitment, but "not every leader has the chops to stick with it."

At Ford's Cleveland Engine Plant No. 2, company and union leadership have stuck with TPM since 1992. The Ford Production System, the automaker's lean production system, "provides a framework of actions and behaviors that support lean manufacturing," said Robert Smillie, plant manager. On a corporate level, the Ford TPM office is a department within the Ford Production System office.

Backbone of Lean

"The foundation of any successful journey toward lean manufacturing is equipment stability, and the best tool to date that manufacturers can use to improve the predictability and stability of their equipment is TPM," he said. The continuous improvement effort helped turn around the plant, which was in danger of closing in the early 1990s.

Smillie described the team structure that supports the successful lean/TPM effort.

A team is typically the entire cross-functional group responsible for manufacturing a component of the engine, or a group associated with a section of the assembly process. Members include machine operators, maintenance trades people, an engineering leader who coordinates the involvement of electrical, mechanical, and tool engineers, and a team manager who oversees the department. Team managers have the discretion of hosting pizza parties, steak dinners, and similar events when the entire team has reached a significant milestone.

Plant objectives are cascaded down to team-level measurements that the teams measure quarterly and compare to past quarters.

Teams access the engineering expertise they need through a central engineering office. A central maintenance office provides additional equipment maintenance expertise. It also is responsible for maintaining the physical plant, construction, and environmental programs, Smillie explained. A predictive/preventive group of tradespersons responsible for infrared analysis, oil analysis, and vibration analysis is an important subgroup within central maintenance.

Don't Neglect the "Soft" Side

A Ford total productive maintenance (FTPM) steering committee, cochaired by labor and management, meets monthly to ensure that TPM principles are adhered to and that FTPM is delivering results. A typical steering committee meeting will deal with plant-wide issues. In addition, small groups regularly address the steering committee about their progress and problems. Smillie said there are about 20 small groups in production.

Like teams, small groups are cross-functional. They draw on experts from the centralized departments as needed. Coordinators from a central FTPM department attend small group meetings, help collect and analyze data, and coach groups along the improvement process. This centralized group also gathers and reports plant-wide measures to management and the TPM steering committee. The coordinators meet weekly with the maintenance supervisors to discuss preventive maintenance (PM), review oil usage and losses, and work on refining the PM tasks to reduce costs.

Smillie, too, warned that organizations spent most of their training on the "hard side" of improvement efforts and not enough time on the "soft" or people side of the business.

One of the most successful soft programs at the plant is the Excellence in Action Rewards and Recognition Program. Employees submit a written form to nominate their peers, either individually or as teams, for the quarterly award.

Employees are nominated for performing "over and above" what management would normally expect in the areas of effort, productivity, innovation and ingenuity, leadership, involvement, safety, and quality.

All the nominations are read during the session in the plant cafeteria. "It's an emotional meeting," said Smillie.

Everyone nominated receives a plaque. Winners receive a lapel pin. "The people who have those pins hold them in high regard because they are not just given away," he noted.

TAKEAWAYS

- Cultural change will follow the actions you take.
- One-point lessons can be effective tools.
- Demonstrating how TPM and lean support corporate strategy will build management support.

14

The "P" in TPM: "Productive" Means "People"

December, 2001

When supporters praise a total productive maintenance program (TPM), they usually talk about how it helps their company make the workplace cleaner and reduces downtime.

The program developed since 1999 at the Parker Abex NWL plant in Kalamazoo, Mich., has certainly done that – and Rich Soderquist, the man in charge of the program, is quick to say so. But Soderquist prefers to talk first about what the program has done for the company's employees.

"Morale seems to be one of the huge benefits – and a clean working environment," he says. "Probably one of the main benefits is instantaneous recognition for employees. They know their work order is going to get recognized now. Everybody's pet peeve is people who don't follow through. They're seeing a lot of follow-through, and that encourages them."

Soderquist says that implementation of TPM – as part of a broader effort to implement lean production – is a big deal. It doesn't just involve keeping the plant cleaner; it requires a complete cultural change in how a company looks at maintenance.

"We wanted to get a maintenance program going because we were so lacking with any kind of preventive maintenance," he explains.

"We were strictly a breakdown mentality. We were constantly chasing our tail."

A New Mandate

Parker Abex is a division of Parker Hannifin, a Cleveland-based maker of hydraulic and pneumatic systems with nearly $6 billion in sales. The Abex division, consisting of the one, 40,000-square-foot plant in Kalamazoo, makes hydraulic power components and distribution systems, primarily for commercial aircraft. Sister divisions in Irvine, Calif., and Ogden, Utah, also serve the aerospace industry.

"Parker in general has a mandate for continuous improvement and lean thinking strategies," Soderquist notes. That direction started coming from the corporate level about in 1996, and Abex began actively pursuing lean processes about a year later.

Soderquist notes that the mandate comes not just from corporate headquarters. "Really, the markets are driving this lean initiative," he says. Parker Abex serves Boeing, which pushes its suppliers to be lean. Parker Abex subsequently seeks lean initiatives from its own suppliers.

So the division started lean efforts, putting on kaizen events – and was achieving benefits. But about in 1999, Soderquist's boss, Jim Skolasky, spoke with him about expanding the efforts because "we were missing the maintenance aspect of it."

One of the first moves in that direction didn't involve people, but a decision to purchase technology. "Our system was just lacking," Soderquist says, so the company starting looking at buying computerized maintenance management software (CMMS). Parker Abex purchased and went live in December 2000 with MP2 6.0 from Datastream – which was also a big deal.

"I really think we were a little naïve as to how much [TPM and the software] would go hand in hand," he comments. "I don't think the company realized how big of a computer program they were purchasing."

The software helps develop preventive maintenance schedules and "eliminates a lot of the guesswork in maintenance," he adds. The company also purchased a sister program, WebLink, which allows any person on the shop floor to write a work request. Such a request automatically goes to a maintenance supervisor.

In 2000, Soderquist – who had held a position in quality and maintenance – assumed the title of TPM program administrator, which also makes him database administrator for the CMMS.

Uncharted Territory

But TPM program administration was the more challenging part of the job, Soderquist notes, because "we didn't have any idea how to implement a TPM program." So Soderquist and others took courses, purchased books and began holding TPM workshops with cross-functional teams of plant employees.

Part of the effort involved working – successfully – with the plant's union, getting it to agree that floor operators could perform certain routine maintenance tasks, such as cleaning, lubricating a machine or tightening a loose bolt.

The workshops achieved significant gains, Soderquist contends. "We would look at equipment, come up with visual controls for it, eliminate any unnecessary circuitry or bad parts – any kind waste we can look at, we'll eliminate that waste."

Much equipment in the plant is 20 to 25 years old, he says; some was refurbished, some was replaced.

Soderquist says he is still working to quantify the benefits the program is achieving. But he says there have been significant reductions in downtime. "For instance, on one test stand, it was taking 30 to 50 minutes to change filters. Now it's just a couple of minutes."

Also, "we take OEE (overall equipment effectiveness) standards and measure. We're trying to show the availability of the machine. If it's running three shifts, maybe we need a new machine. If it's only 14 hours a month, only on the first shift, we can offer customers more use of it."

Epoxy layers on floors have helped eliminate unsafe conditions. And the company has begun using infrared thermography, which takes an infrared photograph that reveals when a machine is operating at an unusually high temperature. "You could tell instantly if a fuse is going bad," Soderquist says, "and you're able to prevent heat loss in a building." Some insurance companies will offer lower rates when this technology is used, he adds.

Some high-level maintenance, such as machine calibration, is being outsourced, and in some cases the outside maintenance company is providing training to plant employees. "We will only deal with people willing to come in and work with union personnel," Soderquist notes.

(The company is sticking by its lean programs in the current economic downturn. Because of the economy, "we've lost 11 employees [out of about 700]," Soderquist says, "but we believe our lean initiatives and lean thinking have kept us from losing more.")

All About People

Soderquist stresses that the real keys to success of a TPM program lie in learning how to work with employees.

For example, when a team develops an action-item list for a particular operation, "we try to keep it under 10 items. We found that if we get too many action items, they don't get done, and that breeds discontent with the employees. When the list is smaller, it seems to build momentum, and we can keep the good stuff going."

In addition, at least two of the items must be preventive maintenance actions. Why? "We find that if we don't set a number, then we never get anything done. We get people who are wishy-washy. We make it a point that we're going to get at least two. It avoids inaction. So many people are willing to put stuff on the back burner," Soderquist says.

A key philosophy is that "we take into account the operator's ideas. Parker Abex feels the operator will be the best source of ideas.

Employee recognition is critical. For example, certificates are given to employees who complete training programs, and the program is listed as corporate training in their personnel records. "That gives them a credential they can take to another employer. Everybody's asking for that in interviews," he says.

Parker Abex also gives special recognition to one key person per quarter. An employee is eligible for the award if they are praised by co-workers. The winner receives a plaque and is publicly recognized at a monthly "all-hands" meeting.

Soderquist encourages others launching TPM programs to "go in baby steps and do a little at a time, and it will pay off."

"It's not a cookbook deal," he stresses. "It's never the same at any two companies, and you need to develop your own program based upon the employees at your company. It's very important to get input as it goes along. Too many people are not flexible. Getting the employee involvement is the key. If they can see movement forward, reaching goals, you're more apt to change the whole culture. And that's really what you're after."

TAKEAWAYS

- Improved morale can be one of the biggest benefits of TPM.
- TPM and computerized maintenance management software go hand-in-hand.
- Teams should be encouraged to develop short lists of improvements items that must include some maintenance items.

15

Visibility and Commitment Sustain TPM at Kodak

August, 2003

It takes several years to change corporate culture. And to success-fully win the hearts and minds of employees, converting them to a new way of thinking, a company must continually publicize its continuous improvement efforts and recognize workers for their achievements.

That's the philosophy of the total productive maintenance (TPM) program at Kodak, as described at Productivity's 2003 TPM Conference by David Frye, manager of the program for Kodak's health imaging division.

The topic of Frye's presentation was "Sustaining TPM," and his focus was on the public visibility of improvement efforts.

"The idea is to make it easy for supervisors and managers to see if (the program) is being carried out," Frye says.

For example, Kodak produces what it calls a "kaizen newspaper" that lists what has been done and what follow-up is required. This is posted in a hallway "where managers walk past." Also promi-nently displayed is a TPM checklist for the operators of each shift. "It's very visual, showing whether or not it has been done," Frye notes.

Equally visible is Kodak's recognition of employee accomplish-

TPM Newspaper

Team Number: _____   Completion Date: 9/6/2002   Page: _1_ of: _____

Item No.	Description of Problem	Counter Measure	Person Responsible	Due Date	% Complete Chart	Date Complete	% Complete
1	Loose Guard	Replace Fastener	J. Smith	10/6/2002			0
2				10/6/2002			25
3				10/6/2002			50
4				10/6/2002			75
5							100
6							
7							
8							
9							
10							
11							
12							
13							
14							

Tracking the status of projects through a publicly posted "TPM Newspaper" is one technique used at Kodak.

ments, which are typically highlighted at team meetings. An associate may receive a verbal thank-you, or a "Good Catch" certificate for solving a particular problem.

There may also be small awards, such as pens and pencils, Frye says, but Kodak shies away from cash rewards.

"The thing that we found with money reinforcement is that, after a while, everybody runs better, so they don't get that reinforcement any more — and they look at that as a takeaway," he explains.

The Long Haul

Underlying Kodak's approach is a particular view of human nature.

"For an individual to change their behavior — quit smoking, lose weight — takes about a year before it becomes natural," says Frye.

A checklist showing which TPM activities have been completed is publicly displayed inside a Kodak health imaging plant.

"It takes three to five years before it's ingrained in an organization." That explains the need for his position, because "you need some external catalyst to keep you on track until it becomes the norm," he adds. He also believes that using external consultants can be worthwhile.

In a similar vein, he observes that "the areas I've seen fail within Kodak are the ones where management loses focus and pulls away the resources necessary to keep TPM going. We train what we call TPM coordinators, kind of a catalyst within a local area to keep this moving. We implement, we see these great gains, and managers say now that we've got great gains, we don't need the TPM coordinator any more and they pull him back into the workforce. There have been times we had a TPM coordinator in place for two years, and we're getting good results, and they are consistent results, so a decision is made to pull the TPM coordinator out. And because it hasn't been three to five years, we begin a downward spiral."

Actually, it hasn't really been three to five years anywhere in Kodak. The company was pushing to implement autonomous maintenance in the 1980s, but "then it kind of went away," Frye recalls. He was promoted into his current position only two years ago in, 2001; some of the seven manufacturing sites for the health imaging division have been pursuing TPM for two years, while others are just getting started.

The sheer size of Kodak creates a challenge to implementing and sustaining any continuous improvement program. One health imaging plant in Colorado employs 350, and there are six other sites within the division. Overall, Kodak has more than 40,000 employees in 11 countries.

Frye sits on a TPM council with counterparts in other divisions. "We're trying to set a common direction for the company," he notes.

Building Buy-In

Training and teamwork are linchpins of the TPM program — along with some healthy competition. "We do share at team meetings. We show the kinds of things other employees have discovered," Frye comments. TPM is "the most powerful team-building activity I've ever seen," he adds. "It's the only tool that truly builds a winning and inclusive culture." He adds, "when people come from other sites to see how we've done things, we include the operators. They like the public recognition."

Frye believes that employees want to be productive and do a good job. He explains: "As part of the training that I give, I ask the operators whether they are more tired at the end of record production, or more tired at the end of a shift spent fighting equipment. Every time, it's the latter."

One of the biggest challenges is "getting the first-line supervisors and lower-level managers to make the leap of faith to actually turn loose control to the employees," Frye says. But he also notes "if management is on board, it's not hard to get the shop floor to do it."

Frye advises those pursuing a TPM program to "benchmark every opportunity you get to see how you're doing." In addition, "whenever you do an event, publish the results."

TPM is just one of a broad spectrum of lean practices and tools that make up what is called the Kodak Operating System. Level loading, heijunka, kanban, visual controls, 5S, poka-yoke — all are part of the Kodak way of life.

That approach is not just a desire for top performance; it's a matter of survival, Frye believes.

He comments, "we hit this in training: In the global economy now, because we are a worldwide manufacturing entity, if we don't do a better job, the jobs will go away. In my opinion, in U.S. manufacturing, unless you're in a niche market, the people that aren't doing TPM and lean manufacturing aren't going to be in business. We don't have the death grip on the market that we did in the '50s and '60s."

TAKEAWAYS

- Continually publicizing TPM efforts and recognizing achievements are key to sustaining the initiative.
- Changing corporate culture may take three to five years.
- Management must stay focused and provide the necessary resources on an ongoing basis.

Part III

Using OEE Effectively

OVERVIEW

One of the most significant and most widely used metrics in connection with TPM is OEE – overall equipment effectiveness. Understanding not only how to calculate OEE but also how to use it appropriately is an ongoing challenge.

Chapter 16, in a straightforward, question-and-answer format, covers several key questions regarding application of OEE, ranging from the number of pieces of equipment it should cover to its use for an entire value stream.

In Chapter 17, common misconceptions about OEE and how it can be misinterpreted are addressed. This thoughtful discussion also focuses on the importance of determining the purpose of OEE in any given situation.

Similarly, Chapter 18 – originally published as a "Lean Advisor Q&A" column – discusses application of OEE to bottleneck vs. non-bottleneck machines, as well as the fact that it may not make sense to apply OEE in all cases.

Chemical company Hercules takes an unusual approach, going beyond OEE with the concept of asset utilization. Chapter 19 explains how to calculate this alternate metric, and how Hercules uses it as a core driver of improvement.

Practical OEE Answers

April, 2001

We recently posed some real-life questions about Overall Equipment Effectiveness (OEE) to Robert Chiarlanza, director of TPM Consulting at Productivity, Inc.

For the uninitiated, OEE is a metric used in implementing Total Productive Maintenance to evaluate how well equipment is used. OEE is the product of three ratios as its formula shows: OEE = availability rate x performance rate x quality rate. The availability rate expresses losses due to unplanned stoppages, the performance rate expresses losses due to machine performance lower than ideal or standard operating rates, and the quality rate expresses losses due to rejects and rework. Collecting and analyzing OEE data is the basis of a systematic approach to reducing equipment-related losses.

Is it better to use OEE on a single machine or a group of machines within a single cell?

OEE should only be used on one piece of equipment within a process. The goal is to elevate the piece of equipment until it is no longer the constraint and then move on to the next constraint in the process. This allows you to focus your resources.

Should OEE be used as a regular performance measurement or as a temporary driver to improvement? Or is this an unnecessary distinction?

OEE is difficult to use as a measurable because often it is compared to some other piece of equipment that is completely different. Also, there is the issue of increasing the speed of equipment. The OEE number, when re-calculated at the new higher speed, could actually be lower than the previous number. When I was working at Visteon's North Penn Electronics Facility, in Lansdale, Pa., we had to report out the OEE on our constraint process. Along with this, we added the output per hour and the number of times the constraint was elevated. The reason was that reporting the output number showed that we were continuously making improvement, because when we moved to the next constraint the OEE number would often decrease. Showing the increase in the number of constraint equipment elevated confirmed that we were moving downstream in the process. Our goal was to have the last piece of equipment in the process, which was usually test equipment, to be the final constraint.

How can OEE be used as a performance measure for an entire value stream rather than a particular cell or machine within the value stream?

It is not a good idea to use OEE for an entire value stream. You'll be wasting too much effort collecting data. But if you do not have a choice, I would recommend using Total OEE. The formula change is simple. Just calculate the availability as if the machine were being utilized for 24 hours a day no matter what the actual scheduled time is. Remember, you are now measuring capacity and not equipment effectiveness.

Related to the previous issue is the question, To what extent is the value stream OEE really reflected in the OEE at the primary constraint?

The value stream cannot produce any more than the constraint equipment allows it to. If your OEE is fairly high and your equipment is not your constraint, or if you are running to takt time, you may want to focus on the total reliability of the line. It is not uncommon to slow equipment down so that it runs to takt time. I would suggest that OEE not be used on the entire value stream in this case. Instead, tracking mean time to repair and mean time to failure would be more meaningful. This is called Reliability Growth.

TAKEAWAYS

- Using OEE as a regular measurable is difficult.
- OEE should be used to measure a single machine, not an entire value stream.
- For a value stream, measuring mean time to repair and mean time to failure may be more meaningful.

17

In Measuring OEE, Higher Is Not Always Better

John Monaco
January, 2000

The purpose of measuring overall equipment effectiveness (OEE) is to drive improvement in the production process. But for OEE to meet this goal it's critical that the people using OEE – or any measure for that matter – understand why they are making the measurement and what is going to happen with the information collected. The leadership must understand it, too, and clearly communicate to operators their expectations and intentions. If you don't take this very critical step, the measure could impair your improvement effort instead of driving it.

Understanding OEE starts with disabusing people of the common fallacy that a high OEE is always good and a low OEE is always bad. When you look at OEE, the real issue is not how high or low it is, but whether or not operators, managers, supervisors, engineers, and technicians understand why the number is where it is.

For example, an OEE of 33 percent may be exactly where you should be to operate effectively. Hopefully, you know why it is at 33 percent. Then, if you want to do something about it, you can look at your value stream map and determine what to improve to increase it. That's a lot different than just hammering people to raise the number from 33 to 50. You really need to know why the number is where it is.

Some people are perfectly content with OEE numbers below the generally accepted world-class rate of 85 percent. They are content because their customers are satisfied. Their production lines are operating to takt time. Therefore, output matches demand. Their machine cycle time has been designed to satisfy takt time. They may not run some of the time, so they may never be above 33 percent or 50 percent because the number is driven by their demand.

Other people may change the OEE equation (OEE = availability x performance rate x quality rate) and only count the time needed to run. For instance, they may decide demand requires them to run only six hours a day. So, they only measure OEE within those six hours. There are all kinds of OEE variations. But the key is intellectual honesty and consistency in how your organization defines OEE.

Most manufacturers, on the other hand, focus OEE on the bottleneck areas. I don't know anybody who has hundreds or thousands of machines who is measuring OEE on every single machine. You should identify the machines causing you the most difficulty, the "gates" that determine the operation's output. Measure those.

Financial Incentive

Generally, you chase the bottleneck around the process. When you improve one bottleneck, something else becomes the bottleneck. If you have cleared all of the bottlenecks and cannot satisfy demand, then that is the time to consider if you need more machines. That is part of the power of OEE. By improving areas with low numbers that get in the way of output, you can defer capital investment. Deferred capital investment is a wonderful way to save money for any organization. It can become a financial incentive to calculate OEE.

Another financial incentive comes from understanding the real costs of downtime. The real cost is the cost of product not made, i.e., an opportunity cost. Then, equipment downtime can be hundreds or thousands of dollars per hour. The cost of equipment downtime can be astronomical for some organizations. For instance, a semiconductor manufacturer told me it is on the order of two million dollars an hour.

Having worked with many organizations, I can tell you that the key for effectively using OEE is to make sure people understand why we make the OEE measure. Don't get hung up insisting that it be a high number. Remember, you are taking the measure to understand what is going on, what are the problems, and what you must do to resolve them.

Sometimes, the problems are painfully obvious. Other times, they are not. The beauty of OEE is that it links availability, performance, and quality. Often, to improve quality, people will slow down a machine or take longer to adjust it. This all impacts availability and/or performance. Quality goes up, but the OEE either stays the same or goes down. This may not be a problem, until you get into a capacity issue and must consider how to get more product out the door. If you are running the machine slower than it could run because you don't understand all of the issues that impact the performance, then you will spend capital dollars when you do not need to.

The Calculation Debate

Some practitioners recommend that you count all the time as available time. But others allow deductions from availability by subtracting time for meetings and other nonproductive activities. Which is right? The answer depends on your objectives.

Supposing you are measuring a 24-hour day, running three shifts. How do you account for all the machine time? If you back out all the meeting time, planned maintenance time, etc., the OEE will show that when you run, you do a helluva job. You just don't run very much because you're always in meetings or performing planned maintenance. The OEE looks good (high), but you cannot satisfy demand.

The purpose of measuring OEE is to understand why you can't get the output you need. If it is an availability issue, then you must consider methods to improve uptime such as changeover reduction activities or autonomous maintenance. You must understand why this machine is not producing enough product.

Consider planned down-time for changeover. Let's say, a plant plans to spend two hours on a changeover and leadership believes it doesn't have to worry about it since it is not in the OEE equation.

However, they still are giving away machine time. The problem I have with the impact of long changeovers arises when demand goes up. You are unprepared. Now, you want to use those hours, but you cannot because you are changing over. The OEE measure as you had constructed it was not giving you an incentive to improve, but it made you look good.

I become wary whenever I hear people say they don't worry about availability because they do maintenance on weekends or changeovers on the back shift when equipment is idle. You can build that expense into your product, but suppose the competition does not? Suppose the competition learns how to do changeovers in less time? Their costs will go down, and you will be in trouble. If demand goes up, you will really be in trouble.

Buy Time, Not Equipment

Sometimes you can run a cell or a line to takt time and calculate OEE on a critical piece of equipment, but never have an 85 percent OEE rate. That can be perfectly acceptable for now because there is low demand. But – the "but" for me is always the same — what if demand goes up?

Sometimes competitors have trouble. You don't wish it on them, but it happens. People have strikes, fires, and financial problems. They cannot deliver to the customer, who then comes to you. If you do not know how to capture the needed time on a piece of equipment, if you do not know why your OEE is where it is, you are in trouble. You may go out and buy new equipment to satisfy what might be a temporary spike in demand. When the demand goes away you are in trouble because the piece of equipment does not go away.

The issue comes back to the question of what is the purpose of OEE. The purpose is to drive improvement on equipment. Understanding why the OEE is where it is, is far more important than driving it to a high number. Mature implementations will, in general, be able to drive critical processes to high numbers. They know where the bottlenecks are and have a cadre of people driving the continuous improvement process. At this point, they may not measure OEE any longer because their focus is continuous improvement.

100 Percent Wrong

Sometimes people report performance over 100 percent. Most likely, they did not know what the theoretical or ideal cycle should be on a piece of equipment and chose some variation of the accounting standard. They make some improvements, and begin getting performance rates above 100 percent.

But you cannot be above 100 percent. Performance is the most common place where you get numbers over 100 percent. A lot of people don't react to that because they are used to efficiency measures above 100 percent. But this is not an efficiency measurement. You must remember that none of these numbers – whether availability, performance or quality – can be above 100 percent. If they are over 100 percent, you must examine the reasons why and determine the next stretch goal for improvement.

Let's say you do not know what the theoretical performance number should be. What do you do? Is there a practical solution? One way is to do what one of my clients did: He had absolutely no idea what the performance number should be. Machines had been in place for 40 years. They had added pumps, conveyors, changed pressures, and switched from relay logic to PLCs as they moved toward computer-controlled systems. How do you determine the theoretical number on a process that has evolved over 40 years?

They did have a history of output. When we examined it, we found that during about 20 days of the year the output of the line was substantially higher than all the other days. We set that as our theoretical output number.

In effect, we were asking, Why can't we get every single day to be just like that? When we get there, we will rethink the number. If you do not rethink it, you distort the equation. Allowing 110 percent or 120 percent to be in there makes your OEE look good. Equipment performance may be fine, but availability may be awful and you would not know it. Your OEE now is insensitive to one of its three components. Don't let that happen. It won't if you remember that everyone in the organization must understand that the purpose of OEE is to drive continuous improvement.

TAKEAWAYS

- Understanding why the OEE number is where it is can be more important than having a high number.
- Whether you deduct certain periods when counting available time depends on your objectives.
- OEE cannot be above 100 percent.

18

Changing the Purpose Of Measuring OEE

Richard J. Niedermeier
September, 2002

Is overall equipment effectiveness (OEE) a useful measurement for a machine that is not a bottleneck?

The basic assumption built into OEE is that the machine being measured is a bottleneck, meaning the speed and capacity of this machine determines — or limits — your production rate. The purpose of OEE, in such a case, is to identify ways to maximize its throughput. If that is the case, the calculation is relatively straightforward.

When the machine is not a bottleneck, you don't need to increase its capacity. But OEE can still be useful in identifying ways to eliminate waste and reduce the cost of operation.

OEE is made up of three components. The first is resource availability. The second is the percentage of production performance to standard output. The last value measures the quality metrics of yield. It is the first component where the "less-than-maximum load" should be reflected.

Normally, the "available time" baseline for a bottleneck machine consists of total shift hours minus breaks and other scheduled lost time.

Table 1: OEE Element No. One: Availability

Scheduled Production Hours	Unplanned Downtime Hours	Hours of Slow Running*	Total Clock Hours	Divisor Hours for Calculation	Availability Percentage
4	2	0	6	6	66.6%
4	0	2	6	4	100%
4	2	2	8	6	66.6%

Table 2: OEE Element No. Two: Performance Rate

Scheduled Production Hours	Unplanned Downtime Hours	Hours of Slow Running*	Total Clock Hours	Divisor Hours for Calculation	Availability Percentage
4	2	0	6	4	100%
4	0	2	6	6	66.6%
4	2	2	8	6	66.6%

With a non-bottleneck resource, the available time is calculated differently. The 100 percent available hours will be the same as the production schedule's loaded production hours for the machine. (Be sure that these hours are consistent with the engineering standards required to produce the quantity scheduled and are the same standard used to calculate the production rate standard in the second component of OEE.) What changes here is that you are now measuring the health of the machine compared to its planned uptime.

Is the machine available when it is scheduled to run? If the machine is run for the hours scheduled and no more, then the availability will be 100 percent. When the resource needs to run extra hours to produce the same quantity, the availability will still be 100 percent, as that is the maximum value for any of the three elements of OEE. The loss in the production rate will be picked up in the second component of OEE. To take account for it in the first component would distort the machine's actual contribution to the value stream.

Availability is equal to operating time divided by net available time. Table 1 shows three scenarios for non-bottleneck machines, and in each, the scheduled production time of four hours is used as operating time. The scenarios on the first and third lines include two hours of unplanned downtime; the net available time is therefore six (four plus two). The percentage is four divided by six, or 66.6 percent.

Each of the scenarios on the second and third lines shows two hours when the machine is running slowly. However, this is not included in this calculation; it comes into play when calculating the second element of OEE, performance.

The same scenarios appear in Table 2. While performance rate is sometimes calculated in relation to parts produced, in this case it is calculated by dividing the scheduled production period (four hours in each case) by the total clock hours, this time including the extra time needed for slow running, but not including unplanned downtime.

A separate calculation would be necessary to determine the quality rate (parts run minus defects, divided by parts run). The three percentages are then multiplied together to calculate OEE. With either a bottleneck or non-bottleneck machine, you should strive to achieve an OEE of at least 85 percent.

Remember that OEE should only be measured where it makes sense to do so. Refrain from measuring OEE in areas where it does not contribute to the lean initiative. (For example, measurements of OEE labeled as "plant-wide" values are relatively meaningless.) It is a useful measurement if used for improvement. If it is not, it becomes just another form of waste.

TAKEAWAYS

- OEE may be used for different purposes in different situations.
- "Available time" may be calculated differently for bottleneck vs. non-bottleneck resources.
- OEE should only be measured where it makes sense to do so.

19

Metric Gives Hercules Strength in Seeing and Fighting Losses

July, 2003

Waste — and the opportunity to eliminate it — can be identified through a variety of methods, such as mapping value streams or calculating overall equipment effectiveness (OEE).

Hercules, a Delaware-based manufacturer of specialty chemicals, tracks down areas for improvement by calculating asset utilization (AU). That's a metric that tells the company the extent to which its manufacturing processes fall short of their capabilities. More importantly, calculation of AU tells Hercules where production losses are occurring, so managers know where to target improvements.

In fact, asset utilization is more than just a metric at Hercules. Since its adoption in 1997, it has — by the company's own description — become a core manufacturing improvement driver. The entire company is focused on reducing or eliminating production losses; doing so increases plant capacity, creating an opportunity to increase sales and profits.

Benefits have been real, according to David Brown, who leads reliability and maintenance improvement for Hercules. In information presented at Productivity's 2003 TPM Conference, held in Las Vegas, he notes that Hercules selected six manufacturing processes for extra attention in 2000. As a result of the improve-

Asset Utilization Calculations

Record #1 (12 AM – 8 AM)
Ideal Rate = 1000 units per hour for Product A
Record Period = 8 hours = Actual Hours
Actual Production = 7410 units of Product A

Ideal Hours = 7410 units / 1000 units per hour = 7.41 Ideal Hours

AU = Ideal hours / Actual Hours = 7.41hours / 8 hours = 92.6%
Loss Hours = Actual Hours – Ideal Hours = 8 – 7.4 = 0.6 hours (Document the reasons)
Documented Reasons:
  0.6 hrs = Quality / Production slowed due to raw material quality

Record #2 (8 AM – 4 PM)
Record Period = 8 hours = Actual hours
Actual Production:
  Product A = 1230 Units
  Product B = 4320 Units

Ideal Rate Product B = 1250 Units / hour

Ideal Hours
  Product A = 1230 Units / 1000 Units per hour = 1.23 hours
  Product B = 4320 Units / 1250 Units per hour = 3.46 hours
                       Total = 4.69 Ideal Hours

Au = Ideal hours / Actual Hours = 4.69 / 8 = 58.5%
Loss Hours = Actual Hours – Ideal Hours 0.= 8 – 4.69 = 3.31 hours
Documented Reasons:
  2.00 hrs = Availability / Emergency repairs / Feed Conveyor bearing failure
  1.3 hrs = Transition Loss / Product Changeover

ment efforts, production at these sites averaged 13 percent above 1999 capacity. In overall results, all processes in one division increased asset utilization an average of 4 percent for the year.

In addition, Brown says, "As production (and maintenance) problems are eliminated, plant costs decrease. There are fewer abnormal situations that can lead to safety or environmental incidents.

Record #3 (4 PM – 12 AM)
(Planned down for inventory control)
Record Period = 8 hours
Actual Production = 0
Ideal Hours = 0
Loss Hours = 8 hours
Documented Reasons:
    1.25 hrs = Transition Loss / Shutdown and Clean-out
    6.75 hrs = No Demand / Shutdown for Inventory Control

Calculations for the day:
Report period = 24 hours = Actual Hours
Ideal hours = 7.41 + 4.69 + 0 = 12.10 hours
Asset Utilization = Ideal Hours / Actual Hours = 12.10 hours / 24 hours = 50.4%
Operating Asset Utilization
    = Ideal Hours / [Actual Hours – No Demand Hours]
    = 12.10 / [24 – 6.75] = 70.1%

Loss Hours Report – Category Level
No Demand	= 6.75 Hours
Transition	= 2.55 Hours
Availability	= 2.0 hours
Quality	= 0.6 Hours
Total Losses	= 11.9 hours

Loss Hours Report – Subcategory Level
Inventory Control	= 6.75 hours
Emergency Repairs	= 2.00 hours
Product Changeover	= 1.3 hours
Shutdown & Clean-out	= 1.25 hours
Raw Material Quality	= 0.6 hours
Total Losses	= 11.9 hours

The plant gains the ability to respond to unexpected sales orders, increasing confidence in production promises and affording the opportunity to gain market share. Plant morale increases as operators and mechanics recognize real progress in eliminating recurring problems."

Crunching the Numbers

In some ways, AU is similar to OEE, which notes the effectiveness of a piece of equipment through a calculation including availability, run rate and first-pass quality.

At a chemical manufacturer like Hercules, materials in production often flow directly from one machine into another. That's one reason the company believes it gets greater value out of AU, which measures the entire process, as compared to OEE, which looks at individual pieces of equipment.

In concept, the calculation of AU is relatively simple. Actual production (the number of units produced) is divided by the ideal rate of production; this yields ideal hours, meaning the number of hours it should take to produce that many units. The result is subtracted from the actual time spent to achieve that production, with the result being the losses for that time period.

Asset utilization is calculated by dividing the ideal hours by the actual hours. The result is expressed as a percentage. (See accompanying example on the previous page.)

Possible Pitfalls

To apply this formula in the real world requires diligence and careful attention to detail in several areas.

Ideal Rate. The ideal rate can be determined in at least a couple of ways. One is to look at the design capacity, but Brown says this often includes assumptions for downtime and less-than-optimal rates. Typically, Hercules determines the ideal rate from actual production — the best historical batch time or shift rate for each product.

On that basis, the ideal rate can be revised on occasion. For example, it can be increased if process improvements increase production to the point where it exceeds the existing ideal rate.

In some cases, Brown notes, the ideal rate increased so dramatically that executives concluded the original ideal rate was set too low. He also warns that the ideal rate should not be set so high that it is beyond the ability of operators to measure and account for losses.

Identifying Losses. The true value in the Hercules system comes from the way it identifies where losses occur. The foundation of that system is a database the company created to record and categorize losses.

Operators or supervisors enter data into the system each shift, recording start and end times, and actual production. The system calculates the amount of losses, and the person entering the data records where those losses occurred. These may be equipment problems, electrical problems, issues with materials, maintenance downtime, etc. Training is essential to make sure similar losses on different shifts are recorded the same way.

The database, in operation for about 30 Hercules plants, is standardized on the top level of loss categories, but an individual plant can set up unique sub and detail categories — a capability that Brown considers essential. The database can also be used for both batch and continuous processes. Analysis of the data can then identify where losses occur most often, or where the largest losses occur.

Interestingly, "about one-third of the problems are maintenance failures, and about two-thirds at the typical plant are process issues," Brown notes.

He also states that asset utilization "can help the operator quantify losses in a complex process. Take, for example, a piece of equipment that is down for six hours, but the process can continue to operate at a reduced rate. It may not be obvious to the operator that the real impact on production was a downtime equivalent loss of 2.5 hours of production. Since the database calculates the losses, it makes this impact more apparent."

And in a batch process, in contrast to OEE, he adds, "if a supporting piece of equipment is down, the impact on production may be different than the equipment downtime. It may be that the equipment is not needed until a certain time, so it causes less process downtime than equipment downtime. Or it may be, in batch or continuous processes, that other problems occur during equipment startup, so the process losses are greater than the equipment downtime."

The Demand Factor

Hercules also uses a metric it calls operational asset utilization (OAU). This is the same as asset utilization except that it excludes demand-related losses — in other words, plant shutdowns or production rate limits that are imposed because market demand isn't strong enough to support operating at full capacity.

OAU, Brown says, "is a better measure of plant performance, and its increase can be directly tied to an increase in plant capacity." The difference between AU and OAU "represents available additional capacity for meeting increases in market demand."

He does note that when a "no demand" rate limit is in effect, there have been instances of plants that are having production problems speeding up above the rate limit to make up for those problems. This is not allowed; the plants are told to work at the given rate and no faster, and work to solve the production problems.

Another issue arises when repairs are performed during downtime caused by a lack of demand. The downtime for repairs is backed out of the "no demand" category and accounted for under availability, which Brown says ensures a proper accounting of plant capacity and available production. He comments, "Our goal is to increase OAU, then push to sell the additional capacity. However, we don't want to sell out our ability to perform necessary maintenance!"

When a plant operates at less than full capacity — only one or two shifts, for example — "there is a tendency to enter the loss hours that the operator is aware of, then enter the remaining losses as No Demand," Brown observes. "This limits the usefulness of the data, because the operator is never prompted to look for losses they didn't notice. It is very important to accurately account for the No Demand downtime, to calculate the remaining production loss hours, then to look for the cause."

Staying on Track

Brown stresses that Hercules' use of asset utilization is part of a drive to create "a corporate culture of improvement."

His recommendations for any company seeking to achieve that goal include:

- Capture best practices

- Perform site assessments

- Select areas for improvement

- Set two-year objectives and a six-month tactical plan

- Have a champion for each site who ensures progress and regularly updates the plan

He also recommends translating goals into actions by shop floor personnel; developing measures — for example, the number of pump failures per month; posting progress prominently and updating it weekly, and also posting higher level metrics, such as OAU.

And he constantly reiterates the importance of training so that all people use the system in the same way.

"The most difficult part seems to be having a consistent understanding of how to categorize these losses," he explains. "If the same loss is put in two different categories, you've gained nothing."

TAKEAWAYS

- Asset utilization, which measures an entire process instead of one piece of equipment, can reveal how a process is falling short of its capability.
- Asset utilization may be particularly useful for a process manufacturer.
- Use of the metric requires diligence and careful attention to detail.

Citations

(All articles taken from the *Lean Manufacturing Advisor*)

Chapter 1: "TPM Takes Center Stage at California Chemical Plant" September 2002: Volume 4, Number 4

Chapter 2: "Data Drives Maintenance Effort." April 2004: Volume 5, Number 11

Chapter 3: "TPM Theme: Show Me the Money." March 2003: Volume 4, Number 10

Chapter 4: "You Can Measure the ROI Produced by TPM Efforts." July 2004: Volume 6, Number 2

Chapter 5: "The Right Analysis Process Improves TPM Effectiveness." January 2005: Volume 6, Number 8

Chapter 6: "You Can't Just Ignore Maintenance-Free Parts." September 2003: Volume 5, Number 4

Chapter 7: "Autonomous Maintenance and 5S in a Parks Department." July 2005: Volume 7, Number 2

Chapter 8: "Kaiser Does TPM Wrong, Then Gets It Right." June 2004: Volume 6, Number 1

Chapter 9: "Implementers Offer TPM Tips." August 2000: Volume 2, Number 3

Chapter 10: "Focusing the TPM Effort." March 2000: Volume 1, Number 10

Chapter 11: "Education, Support Drive TPM Success (CME)." June 2002: Volume 4, Number 1

Chapter 12: "Failures & Countermeasures Mark The Real-World TPM Experience." June 2005: Volume 7, Number 1

Chapter 13: "Soft Side Gets Hard Look" October 2000: Volume 2, Number 5

Chapter 14: "The "P" In TPM: "Productive" Means "People"." December 2001: Volume 3, Number 7

Chapter 15: "Visibility and Commitment Sustain TPM at Kodak." August 2003: Volume 5, Number 3

Chapter 16: "Practical OEE Answers." April 2001: Volume 2, Number 11

Chapter 17: "In Measuring OEE, Higher is Not Always Better." January 2000: Volume 1, Number 8

Chapter 18: "Changing the Purpose of Measuring OEE." September 2002: Volume 4, Number 4

Chapter 19: "Metric Gives Hercules Strength In Seeing and Fighting Losses." July 2003: Volume 5, Number 2

Index

Lean Manufacturing Advisor ...

Your Monthly, Independent Source for First-Hand, Current, and Practical Advice.

If the articles in this book are proving helpful, and you want to stay current on the latest trends and developments in lean implementation, then you should subscribe to *Lean Manufacturing Advisor.*

Lean Manufacturing Advisor's editorial team gives you the behind-the-scenes news and advice, and real-life, how-to-implement details from people on the same continuous improvement journey as you. Its in-depth coverage demonstrates how you can be an effective agent of change and lead management and front line employees in a successful lean transformation.

Each month *Lean Manufacturing Advisor* covers the latest developments in lean manufacturing with these unique features:

- Case studies, featuring successful real-life lean initiatives, provide a wealth of ideas to share with your team.

- The Q&A section addresses common technical questions.

- Editorials offer advice, analysis, and commentary on the latest developments in lean manufacturing.

- Photos, diagrams, and samples documents show you what other companies are doing.

When you subscribe to *Lean Manufacturing Advisor,* you join a community of experienced executives and managers who have successfully implemented lean in their organizations. You'll leverage their experience, benchmark your progress, avoid the pitfalls, and speed lean implementation.

Get the insider's view that you can't find on corporate websites or in trade magazines, subscribe to *Lean Manufacturing Advisor!*

To subscribe, visit our website: www.productivitypress.com, or call toll-free at 1-888-319-5852. For multiple subscriptions of 3 or more copies, contact us at ehanus@productivitypress.com.

Printed in the United States
By Bookmasters

Printed in the United States
by Baker & Taylor Publisher Services